God Guy

God Guy

Becoming the Man You're Meant to Be

Michael DiMarco

Revell

a division of Baker Publishing Group
Grand Rapids, Michigan

Hungry Planet

© 2009 by Hungry Planet

Published by Revell
a division of Baker Publishing Group
P.O. Box 6287, Grand Rapids, MI 49516-6287
www.revellbooks.com

Printed in the United States of America

Library of Congress Cataloging-in-Publication Data
DiMarco, Michael.
    God guy : becoming the man you're meant to be / Michael DiMarco.
       p.   cm.
    ISBN 978-0-8007-1941-8 (pbk.)
       1. Teenage boys—Conduct of life. 2. Teenage boys—Religious life. I. Title.
BJ1671.D56 2009
248.8′32—dc22   2009026728

Published in association with Yates & Yates, LLP, Literary Agents, Orange, California.

Interior design by Sarah Lowrey Brammeier
Creative direction by Hungry Planet

Contents

"Live in me,
and I will live in you.

A branch cannot produce
any fruit by itself.

It has to stay
attached
to the vine.

In the same way, you cannot

produce fruit unless

you live in me."

—John 15:4

1

Do You Know a Double G?

I believe that the **God Guy** (occasionally referred to as a Double G) is the **STRONGEST** guy on the planet, not because of what he does but because of who he **WORSHIPS.**

Everything he does is affected by the fact that he knows and is related to the most powerful being in the universe. Because of that he knows where he came from and where he's going. His life isn't perfect; it wasn't meant to be. It's sometimes obnoxious, sometimes loud, and sometimes messy. He has big plans, big hopes,

Do You Know a Double G?

and big prayers. He wants what every other guy wants: respect and acceptance. He wants people to like him and to look up to him. He wants a life of peace. He wants to be a hero. Some days he's on top of the world and nothing can bring him down, and some days he hits bottom, but what makes him different from just any guy is the God he serves. His right relationship with the Creator of the universe. What's a right relationship? Imagine asking God with the most reverent attitude, "We good?" And God responds, "We're good." That's a right relationship. And unlike the average guy, a Double G can admit that he can't do this messed up and crazy life on his own, and he is totally willing to trust that God can. When life is more than he can handle, God is more than he needs.

UNLIKE THE AVERAGE GUY, A DOUBLE G CAN ADMIT THAT HE CAN'T DO THIS MESSED UP AND CRAZY LIFE ON HIS OWN, AND HE IS TOTALLY WILLING TO TRUST THAT GOD CAN.

11

The life of the God Guy is not affected as much by what others think of him or do to him as it is by who God is. He defines his life by the fact that he belongs to God. The most crucial moment in his life was the moment he said, **"Yes, God, I believe."** The second most crucial? When he realized he can't do it alone. It was when the Double G came face-to-face with all power and all strength and didn't run and hide. When Jesus reached out of the pages of that old Bible, grabbed him by the hoodie, and said, "Come with me. Make

HE DEFINES HIS
THAT HE BELONGS

me Lord of your life, and I will be with you always. You will never have to fear again."

Do you remember? Did you say yes, or did you pull away?

I remember when I said yes. I had been searching for a long time for something bigger than me. Bigger than my ego, bigger than my faults, bigger than my shame. I was seventeen when I said I believed, but it was over a decade later when I finally said, "I can't do it alone."

I think I have a pretty lame testimony, because I spent almost fifteen years of my life faking like I was a Christian but living a lie. I'd lie, cheat, steal, and hop from one girlfriend's bed to another, saying, "Well, she's the one, so we might as well."

I lived the life of the nice guy turned bad boy before I realized that God just wanted me to be real and honest, and he'd work on me from there. No frontin', as he may have whispered to me once or twice. And that's when I finally said, "I surrender all, because I

LIFE BY THE FACT TO GOD

finally realize I'm not good at being perfect, but you are." Yeah, I'm quick like that. Instead of just talking a good game, I started to live it and started talking about my *real* life, not the one that a Christian guy was supposed to have. Now I believe *and* freely testify that I mess up daily, with the exception of when I let God stay in control.

God changes lives. There is no question. If he hasn't changed yours, then it's your own fault, not his.

He wants to; you just haven't let him. It's easy to believe that he won't come through, that you'll be duped into believing some lie. But I'm living proof that that isn't true. He was there all along; I just didn't have the facts or purposely ignored them to stay in control or do and get what I wanted.

If you believe that Jesus is who he says he is, then you are a God Guy.

That may or may not have changed your life up to this point, but look out, because we (God and me) are about to rock your world. I believe that if you are reading these words right now, you're reading them for a reason, and it isn't because you are being punished or Granny is trying to fix you by buying you this book. It's because God has something to do in your life. He wants to make you into the man you were created to be. So you've gotta trust that a change is coming and get ready to take the wildest ride of your life.

Searching for More

If you are a God Guy, it's because of who you worship, not who you are or what you've done or failed to do. His reaching out and choosing you changed who you were at the very core. You might not feel it every day, but trust me when I say that it did.

Yet deep down inside you might feel like a failure, like you're not the man you were meant to be. All those missed opportunities, so many wrong decisions. Sure, you're a good guy—you haven't turned your back on him or tried to be a bad guy; you're just human and sinful. That's how the story goes for a lot of us.

But now you want MORE.
You want MORE of him,
MORE of the real you,
MORE FAITH.

It's true what they say, you know, that "there is no one righteous, not even one" (Romans 3:10 NIV). So it should be no surprise that your life might not be exactly what you pictured. And it's good that you want more, because more is exactly what you're gonna get when you take a fearless look at God's Word and are willing to let it shine some light on all your bruises, cuts, bumps, and zits. When you let it into the very center of your thumping heart with all its selfish motives and unmet fantasies,

It's true what they say, you know, that 'there is no one righteous, not even one.' (Rom. 3:10) So it should be no surprise that your life might not be exactly what you pictured.

all its noble hopes and dreams, you set yourself up for a soul renovation. Anyone can benefit from exposing their life to God's Word. And as a guy who wants God's thoughts to be your very own, you cannot fail to open up Scripture and be changed. The only question is, how much change are you willing to go for?

Do you want more of God in your life? More of his love, more of his peace, more of his presence? Do you want to be different than the typical guy who just wants more of God's *presents* like he's Santa Claus? Then strap in and hang on, because that's just what's in store for you. Your natural human tendency is to move, to wander, and to squirm. Staying, or abiding, is often one of the hardest things, but it's that thing that brings the very Christ in whom you abide deeper into your life.

Being the Branch

I want you to imagine a branch, and this branch isn't attached to anything. Not to a tree or a vine. It is connected to nothing bigger than itself.

Can you see it? Laying there all alone, maybe in your backyard?

How long do you think that branch will remain flexible and grow leaves or even fruit? How long till it gets brittle and snaps under the weight of someone's foot? Or before your dog makes like a beaver and chews it to bits?

Remember how I said it took me fifteen years to realize I couldn't do it alone? I was that branch—alone, without anything or anyone bigger than myself, until I realized that I needed to be attached to something stronger, something that would feed me spiritually and emotionally so that I could grow muscle, real spiritual muscle.

Jesus, in the book of John, describes us as branches, but he also describes himself as the vine. And he promises us that if we are willing to remain in him (in other words, stay attached to that something bigger), we will have everything good to show from it. In Galatians, the good—the stuff that grows from a healthy branch that stays attached to the vine—is called fruit. And in human terms it's stuff like this: it's love, joy, peace, patience, kindness, goodness, faithfulness, gentleness, and self-control (see Galatians 5:22–23). It's you at your best. It's everything that you think and do that is good. It's all the stuff that brings glory to God and makes him look amazing in the eyes of others. It's the cool part of your life, and God's main goal is to bring that stuff out of you.

So let's take a quick look at the entire verse about the vine and the branches, shall we? Just to help it sink in, as you read, do this. Put a cross above all the words that stand for Jesus (like *vine*, *I*, etc.). And draw a cloud around all the words that refer to the Father (like *vinedresser*, *he*, etc.). Then underline all the action words (like *removes*, *prunes*, etc.).

[Then Jesus said,] "I am the true vine, and my Father takes care of the vineyard. He removes every one of my branches that doesn't produce fruit. He also prunes every branch that does produce fruit to make it produce more fruit. You are already clean because of what I have told you. Live in me, and I will live in you. A branch cannot produce any fruit by itself. It has to stay attached to the vine. In the same way, you cannot produce fruit unless you live in me. I am the vine. You are the branches. Those who live in me while I live in them will produce a lot of fruit. But you can't produce anything without me. Whoever doesn't live in me is thrown away like a branch and dries up. Branches like this are gathered, thrown into a fire, and burned. If you live in me and what I say lives in you, then ask for anything you want, and it will be yours. You give glory to my Father when you produce a lot of fruit and therefore show that you are my disciples."

John 15:1–8

He is the vine.

The vine is the trunk of the plant. It's the big part that
has all the roots and grows out of the ground.

And the branches are us.

Believers live in him, get our strength and our life
from the trunk, the vine, Jesus.

And the vinedresser is God the Father.

He walks the vineyard and tends to the branches,
pruning them, cutting them and cleaning them. The
vinedresser's main goal is to grow more fruit. The
more the better.

Jesus says that if you live in him

you will bear lots of fruit.
And if you don't live in him then you aren't
going to grow any fruit.

LET'S GET THE picture.

It's a beautiful sunny day in the middle of this huge vineyard. The roots are old and big. They climb up the trellis and shoot out all kinds of branches that are covered with leaves and fruit. The vinedresser is there, and he is tending to his most prized possession, working his hardest to get the most fruit he possibly can out of his plant. He has on his big Italian hat and his dirty work gloves. (Hey, with a name like DiMarco, you know I got to go Italian on you, right? My grandfather even grew grapes and made wine old school with foot stomping and such. But I digress.) He has a big ol' bucket of water and a sponge. He moves across the vineyard, picking up the weak branches that are crawling along the ground

He PRUNES,

He CUTS,

and scrubbing the mold off of them; he rubs off the mud and places them on the trellis high up in the sun so that they can start to grow fruit. He cuts off the smaller shoots, refusing to let them crowd out the fruit that will come on the bigger branches. He prunes, he cuts, and all is done in a powerful yet gentle way that will clean the fruit and help it to get big and fat.

You've gotta understand the job of the vinedresser in order to really get the full impact. His goal is not to stress out the vine or the branches. He's not grabbing the stuff in anger and just pruning willy-nilly, chopping haphazardly. He's not even cutting just to make things look better. He's working with a purpose, and each move he makes has one goal: to improve the production of the plant.

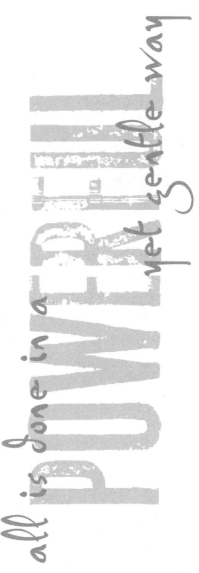

all is done in a POWERFUL yet gentle way

21

WHAT DOES THIS HAVE TO DO WITH YOU?

But what does this dresser of the vino—I mean vine—have to do with you, God, and Jesus?

This scene is the symbol of your life. It's like this: when your life is messed up and you're down in the dark mud, with worms and vermin eating away at your leafy growth, showing all kinds of mold and producing wimpy pieces of fruit if any at all, the vinedresser—God—comes along and cleans you up, lifts you up, and gets you out into the sun. When God forbids you to do stuff but you do it anyway out of weakness or rebellion or just because you can, your branch gets sick, dirty, and weak. And when that happens fruit can't grow. Nothing can. You're not healthy enough to produce anything good, so you get moldy and muddy and weak. And life starts to feel out of control.

But the vinedresser is there working, cleaning, doing his part to increase your fruit. If you look at that list of fruit in the verse you read a minute ago and see any of it lacking in your life, then your fruit production is lower than it could be, and that's when things start to get shaken up. Things get cut and pruned and moved around. And cutting and pruning isn't pretty. It hurts when it's happening to you. But the results can be something incredible if you are willing to let the vinedresser do the work.

A **God Guy,** by definition, is **A GUY CONNECTED TO GOD.** Not a guy who likes God or who is interested in God, not just a homeboy, but one who is *connected* to him.

A God Guy knows that he has to remain attached to the vine, continually getting strength and nourishment from it and never moving away from it. And he knows that being lifted out of the mud and occasionally washed and even pruned is a necessary and good thing.

All this branch and vine talk can sound weird. You hear people talking about abiding in Christ and staying or remaining in him, but what does that mean in your day-to-day life? How do you work that out practically?

Maybe, just maybe that's why this book is in your hands—to help you figure that out. As you read through this book, I'm gonna give you practical ways to stay connected to Christ when it comes to your friends, your family, girls, strangers, and even your enemies. I also hope you learn what it means when it comes to knowing yourself and how to express yourself to the world around you. So let's take a look at the life of a God Guy and see how becoming more like him will change your life for the better.

2

A Guy Who Knows
Love

Dear friends, we must

LOVE EACH OTHER

because *love*
comes from God.

Everyone who loves

HAS BEEN BORN FROM GOD

and knows God.

The person who doesn't *love*

doesn't know God,
because *God is love.*

1 John 4:7–8

My dad is dead.

He died the year before I met my wife, Hayley, so they never met and she and my daughter will never know him except for the stories I tell. And some of those stories are just repeated stories that he told me, because he was almost fifty years old when I was born. He actually fought in World War II. So it's weird when I fire up Call of Duty on the Xbox and know that my dad was there, getting two Purple Hearts and catching a Japanese bayonet in the shoulder.

Most of his war stories he didn't share with me until after I graduated from high school, for a couple of reasons: one, because he knew I'd probably join up like he did, and two, because he hated taking other men's lives. He was an honest and honorable man. He was a war hero. Ladies loved him, but he was fiercely loyal to my mom, and he loved me in the strong, silent sort of way. He never said "I love you" but instead "You know I love you, right?" Hey, worked for me. He was far from perfect; he was overly cautious at times. Like when he wouldn't sign the permission form for me to join the football team because he was afraid I'd get hurt and he didn't really get why sports were so important to me (they were so important that I tried to lie my way onto the team). Or how he hid his "playa" days that I could've learned from and been prepared to avoid. And how he rarely said he was wrong. Worse yet, he left me. He died, and even though I was an adult by then, I still need him today more than ever.

Inside every guy is a longing to have the perfect love and respect relationship with his father. No matter how great or how horrible he actually was as father, we all deeply desire more intimacy with the first man in our lives and long to have him say, "I'm proud of you, son." Your dad, just like mine, will forever be a part of your heart, no matter what he's done or not done. A guy's father is his first mentor, his evidence that there truly is a God who truly loves him and believes in him. I believe that in each of our hearts there is a blueprint that points directly to a pure, untainted love from a father that only one can ever truly fulfill. You might get that feeling when your earthly dad says, "I'm proud of you son" or when he says, "Well done!" But because your dad is imperfect, your earthly father can never be all the love that you need. He is simply your shot at a quick look at the original Father. And no matter what your father was like or is like, no matter how he loved or hated, no

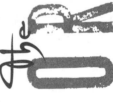

28

matter who your father here on earth is, your Father in heaven truly loves you. He's the reality that a father on earth should be a reflection of.

If your dad wasn't a good reflection of God the Father, I am sorry. I know how you feel, and I'm sorry. But you have to remember that your dad is only human and that the thing that you really want from him—love—is still out there, and it's bigger and better than anything on this whole earth. The Bible says that God not only wants us to love, he is love (see 1 John 4:8). Did you get that? He *is* love. That means he's the Dad unlike any other. He's got your back for eternity. He's never gonna walk out on you or reject you. He knows how to instruct you and encourage you. He wants you to get that, and he even wrote it down, like a contract, a guarantee of his faithfulness, right there for everyone to read. Check it out:

I am convinced that nothing can ever separate us from God's love which Christ Jesus our Lord shows us. We can't be separated by death or life, by angels or rulers, by anything in the present or anything in the future, by forces or powers in the world above or in the world below, or by anything else in creation.

Romans 8:38–39

GOD'S LOVE is here to stay, and for you that means that he will give you the **STRENGTH** you need to be the **MAN** you were made to be.

It means that no matter how wimpy you feel or how messed up your life is right now, **he will never leave you or give up on you** (see Hebrews 13:5). And that's what makes trusting him such a sure thing. When you can know beyond a shadow of a doubt that he is faithful and never walks out, you can feel free to trust him with all your heart, with all your soul, with all your mind, and with all your strength (see Mark 12:30).

Love is the best way to describe God. He is, by definition, **love**; therefore, everything that he does is out of **love**. Everything that he says, thinks, feels—it is all formed in **love**. So that means that **love** is the most important thing in the life of a guy whose goal is to be the example of God's love to the world. Everything else that you will ever do rests on your understanding of his

love. There is no commandment, no rule, no requirement that isn't built on **love**. And that's good news. **Love** is not only the most amazing thing in the world; it is also the foundation of faith. Jesus put it like this:

> "Love the Lord your God with all your heart, with all your soul, and with all your mind." This is the greatest and most important commandment. The second is like it: "Love your neighbor as you love yourself." All of Moses' Teachings and the Prophets depend on these two commandments.
>
> Matthew 22:37–40

love should be the highest goal of the Double G (see 1 Corinthians 14:1). It's his gift to the Creator. It's his way of saying thanks and of respecting and honoring God. It defines the God Guy. "Everyone will know that you are my disciples because of your **love** for each other" (John 13:35). When he **loves**, he obeys the two greatest commandments and so fulfills the rest of them. Love is the passageway into a life of faith, and it returns as much to the guy as it does to God. **Love never disappoints.** You're gonna be rejected, you're gonna hurt, but when you obey God's command to love, you get all kinds of public and secret rewards.

The truth about *love* is that it makes life easier. When you learn to love no matter what the circumstances, you gain the strength to rise above. You gain the muscle of hope and the power of confidence, and your life gets better just because you choose love instead of anger, hate, aggression, or resentment. Love is the fuel of a strong and holy life.

What Does Love Look Like?

But what is love? It is such a massive concept that it can be hard to really know how to do it. So let's take a look at some of the basics of loving God's way in everyday life.

The Double G with His Friends

The God Guy (Double G) with his friends is a good guy (also Double G, yo). He's so tight that no one can hold anything against him. He is fun to be around. He isn't whiny or arrogant; he lives outside of himself. He actually cares about what his friend is going through. He says what he means and he means what he says. He's not fake. His friends trust him and know they can count on him to be there when they need him. He's not hot-tempered or easily ticked off (see 1 Corinthians 13:5). The God Guy looks different than most guys when the world looks at him because he isn't self-obsessed (see Matthew 16:24); he's relaxed and cool. He considers other more important than himself, and it shows in how he treats them (see Philippians 2:3–4). He loves differently than the average dude, and that's because in all his relationships there is the pres-

"If you are **HARD** and **VINDICTIVE,** insistent on your **OWN WAY,** certain that the **OTHER PERSON** is more likely to be in the **WRONG** than you are, it is an indication that there are whole tracts of your nature that have never been transformed by His gaze."

Oswald Chambers (wise dead guy)

HE'S NOT FAKE

HIS FRIENDS TRUST HIM

HE'S NOT HOT-TEMPERED

HE ISN'T SELF-OBSESSED

ence of Jesus. People want to be around him because he makes them feel relaxed and loved. To him, friendship is not about what he can get but how he can be a representation of Jesus in others' lives and so point them to Jesus. And because of that, the God Guy is the best friend another guy can have.

But what happens when things get tough and friendship gets ugly? How does the God Guy deal with a jerky friend? What if his friend is overreacting? How does the God Guy deal with adversity in friendship?

With confidence. The God Guy has confidence in his God and in God's sovereignty (google it if you don't get it), so he never gets too worked up. He doesn't let the emotional life of weaker people affect his life. He doesn't have to fight; he has to *love*. He doesn't demand the loyalty of anyone but himself. And so when things get tough he stays *cool, calm,* and *collected* (triple C, yo). He gives others what they need, not just what they want. Love always puts others first; it's never irritable or vengeful, because it lives for a greater purpose. To love is to be a representative of Christ to the world. So when the God Guy loves, he always puts Christ first, not himself. The God Guy is the best friend the world can have.

You might not feel like the best friend. You may have messed up in the past, but you can't let that determine your future. Love takes practice. You're going to make mistakes, but that's okay. You can't let failure become a reason to give up; make it a reason to try harder. When you love the way God designed you to love, not only will you find more love for yourself, but your life will have less drama and destruction in it. People will be drawn to you, and even if they aren't, you will be okay with that.

So don't let the job ahead of you scare you. Just trust that love is yours to give and that you can be the most amazing friend by the power of the living God.

The God Guy with His Family

Sometimes the hardest people to love can be the ones who are closest to you. I know that I don't get as frustrated with my friends as I do with my mother. And I bet the same might be true for you. But the God Guy has to make an amazing effort to bring peace to his home.

In Jesus's parable of the vine and the branches (see John 15:1–8), he tells us how each one of us who belongs to him are part of the vine. Can you imagine a branch of a plant lashing out and trying to hurt the branch right next to it? It would be like hurting itself. And that's what we do when we fight with our families. We are a part of one another, and we have to love each other.

In fact, you've probably heard it a million times, so let's make it a million and one: you have to "honor your father and your mother, so that you may live for a long time in the land the LORD your God is giving you" (Exodus 20:12). Honor means that you don't argue with them in anger or bitterness. You don't roll your eyes or ignore them, but you give them the **respect** God commands you to give them. You might discuss differences and disagreements with them, but you always respect them as the authority over you, like a boss or a teacher. As a God Guy you are the hands and feet of God even to your family. Each person that you live with has their own story, their own walk. And each one has their own problems. As a God Guy, your **gift of loving them is a gift of protection.**

Home shouldn't be a **WAR ZONE** but a **refuge.** When you love your family, you help it to be that for them, but also for you.

The God Guy loves his family, no matter how crazy or how bad they are, because he knows that God purposed him for this exact family and that his role in it is crucial. He can either be a change agent in their lives and his own, or he can resign himself to powerlessness and anger. But the God Guy always chooses hope, faith, and love. And those choices demand a love that never gives up and always believes. Love your family and you will find love for yourself.

But how does loving your family look? You've probably heard this all before, but have still had your share of family drama. So how about some help. Well, here are some things to think about when it comes to your family:

1. **Ask yourself what God wants to teach you through this person or problem.** Be real: if the same problems happen over and over again, what leads up to them? Trace your steps. Then see if God doesn't want you to change something. Your life will never advance and you will never grow if you aren't willing to look at your problems and take some of the blame—or at least take some action toward making them better.

2. **Apologize.** An apology covers up a lot of problems. When there is a fight, apologize. That means look the person in the eye and say, "I'm sorry." You can surely find something you did wrong. If it will help soften the situation, then just say it. An apology isn't an act of weakness but an act of

strength. Only weak people can't apologize. Your apology elevates you in the mind of the person you apologize to; it doesn't show your weakness. You're also leading by example.

3. **Don't escalate the conflict.** When you are tested, think about your relationship with God. How does he want you to react? This doesn't depend on how the other person is acting but on what would please God. It can be easy to fight back, to shout, and to slam doors, but that never gets you what you want and it never gets God what he wants. Self-control in these situations is power. You want to grow? Then control yourself and don't escalate problems. Be the problem solver, not the problem builder.

4. **Be willing to be wrong.** Jesus never fought back when people accused him of things. He didn't argue. So why do you have to? Be willing to be wrong in someone's eyes, knowing that God knows your heart. Being wrong isn't the worst thing in the world. Confident men aren't afraid to admit they were wrong. The only time your

It can be easy to fight back, to shout, and to slam doors, but that never gets you what you want and it never gets God what he wants. Self-control in these situations is power.

mistake keeps you from succeeding is when you refuse to admit that you made a mistake.

If you want more help on loving your family, check out my wife's book *Stupid Parents*.

The God Guy with Girls

Take a look at how a Double G acts with girls. He isn't shy or fearful. He doesn't cower in their presence. He is strong and confident—not because of who he is but because of who God is and has commanded him to be. God calls you to be strong and courageous (see Deuteronomy 31:6), so to fear a girl is to disobey God.

The God Guy appreciates girls for their differences. He doesn't expect them to be one of the guys, and he understands that their feelings are different from his. He knows girls love romance, so he doesn't use it to control her or to get her, but he gives it when he means it and when they're both mature and committed enough to handle it. He knows how girls think, and he does what he can to avoid leading them on or breaking their hearts. He respects them and his role as their protector. He knows that when he's with a girl, he's not just with her but with God too, so he gives her the honor that God would approve of.

A God Guy appreciates girls for who they are but also knows that he doesn't need a girl in order to be a man. He doesn't define himself based on the number of girls he can get. And he doesn't let girls get in the way of the more important things. He is honest with girls without being cruel. He acts honorably in their presence, and all the girls who know him know that God is his most important relationship.

A God Guy has his **own life** and never lets the life of a girl become his main focus. He knows that if he did, he would be removing God from that rightful and lofty position and also making himself weak in the eyes of the girl. One of the reasons girls go for bad boys is because bad boys never worship girls; they always have lives of their own and keep a safe emotional distance from girls. I'm not recommending the way of the bad boy—just illustrating what draws girls to them. The God Guy knows that making a girl his main focus actually chases her off and doesn't give her what she craves.

The God Guy is honest with girls about guys. He wants to protect them from bad guys, so he never argues the fact that average guys are sexual beings. He might have total control of himself, but he knows that many other guys don't, so he wants to protect girls and not give them a false sense of security. He has no problem saying to a girl, "Most guys are dogs" and "Make any guy you think is worthy consistently prove that he's not." That's because

Love is an ACTION, not a feeling.

How can you be sure that love isn't a feeling? Simple. God commands you to love. And since feelings can't be commanded, love can't be a feeling. See, I can't order you to be miserable right now; it's not possible to turn on those kinds of feelings. But actions can be commanded. I can command you to stand on one foot, and you could easily do it (at least I hope so). So, if God is commanding you to love, he isn't talking about how you feel about someone but about what you do for them. Love is an action, not a feeling.

HE KNOWS HOW VALUABLE

a girl's heart is

and he wants to guard it for her, keeping her from falling for weak or manipulative guys.

When a God Guy loves a girl, he protects her and cares for her. He loves her the way God does—not with a possessive love but with a love that gives her freedom and trusts that if God wants them together, it'll all work out, but their personal relationships with God are more important to their happiness than their relationship with each other.

So when it comes to love and girls, the God Guy lives like this:

1. He doesn't ever choose the love of a girl over his relationship with God (see Galatians 1:10).
2. He guards her heart and doesn't use romance to manipulate her (see Proverbs 4:23).
3. He isn't jealous (see 1 Corinthians 13:4).
4. He doesn't depend on a girl to be his source of happiness, but instead depends on God (see Galatians 5:22).

5. He never idolizes a girl (see Exodus 20:4).

6. He never fights over a girl (see Matthew 5:44).

The God Guy with His Enemies

Love by its very nature isn't picky. And that means that you don't give it just to the lovable but offer it to the unlovable as well. If you only love those who love you back, then what good is love to a world that is dying? Jesus asks, "If you love those who love you, do you deserve a reward? Even the tax collectors do that! Are you doing anything remarkable if you welcome only your friends? Everyone does that!" (Matthew 5:46–47). Love can't exclude people who don't love you back—in other words, jerks, losers, haters, idiots, and the rest. It's for everyone, even your enemies. Jesus makes that clear when he says, "But I tell you this: Love your enemies, and pray for those who persecute you" (Matthew 5:44).

CAN YOU DO IT? CAN YOU LOVE SOMEONE WHO IS OUT TO GET YOU?

Someone who wants to hurt you? If not, Jesus asks, then what good is your love? The God Guy doesn't love because of who others are or what they do but because of who God is and what he has done.

Three days before Hayley and I got married, an old boyfriend of hers actually drove across the country to get her to postpone the wedding. Not only that, but it was my birthday. Let me tell you, I wanted to pummel the guy. But our Father has different instructions: "Don't repay evil for evil. Don't retaliate with insults when people insult you. Instead, pay them back with a blessing. That is what God has called you to do, and he will bless you for it" (1 Peter 3:9 NLT). Now, in this case, the biggest blessing I could give the guy was to *not* pummel him; I didn't even say "boo" to him. Not the best blessing in the world, but far better than my past habit of throwing down at a moment's notice.

The point is, the God Guy defines himself by his God and not by the actions of others. Therefore, he is never a victim. He never feels a need to over-power mean people or run from them, because he sees their actions as an opportunity to prove that God is more important than anything anyone else could throw at him. Mean people were an essential part of his salvation, because hate and anger were what put Christ on the very cross that saved him. Mean isn't a surprise to God, and for the God Guy it's an opportunity for a new life and a chance to prove the power of love.

So when you find yourself with enemies in your life, you have to choose to be like Christ, who "never verbally abused those who verbally

THE GOD GUY DEFINES HIMSELF BY HIS GOD AND NOT BY THE ACTIONS OF OTHERS.

SELFLESS *Love?*

Lately, my Father has revealed to me a depth of selfishness in myself that I never even so much as suspected. I find that all my kindness to others, my benevolence, and what seemed to be the most unselfish acts of my life, all have had their root in a deep and subtle form of self-love. My motto has for a long time been "Freely ye have received, freely give" and I dreamed that in a certain sense I was living up to it, not only as regards physical blessings, but spiritual as well.

But I find now that I have never really given one thing freely in my life. I have always expected and demanded pay of some kind for every gift, and where the pay has failed to come, the gifts have invariably ceased to flow. If I gave love, I demanded love in return; if I gave kindness, I demanded gratitude as payment; if I gave counsel, I demanded obedience to it, or if not that, at least an increase of respect for my judgment on the part of the one counseled; if I gave the gospel, I demanded conversions or a reputation of zeal and holiness; if I gave consideration, I demanded consideration in return. In short I sold everything, and gave nothing. I know nothing of the meaning of Christ's words "Freely ye have received, freely give." But I did it ignorantly.

Now however the Lord has opened my eyes to see something of the nature and extent of this selfishness, and I believe He is also giving me grace to overcome it in a measure. I have been taking home to myself the lesson contained in Matthew 5:39–48. I desire to do everything now as to the Lord alone, and to receive my pay only from Him. His grace must carry on this work in me for I am utterly powerless to do one thing toward it; but I feel assured that He will.

And I feel have to thank Him for what He has already done. He has conquered a feeling of repugnance which was growing in me towards someone with whom I am brought into very close contact, and enabled me to give freely, without even wanting any return. Oh how great He is in strength and wisdom!

—*The Christian's Secret of a Holy Life: The Unpublished Personal Writings of Hannah Whitall Smith* abused him. When he suffered, he didn't make any threats but left everything to the one who judges fairly" (1 Peter 2:23). Christ is your example, so don't be surprised when people hate you, but instead trust your life to the God who never disappoints.

The Double G with Strangers

The strength of a God Guy is never more evident than when he is with strangers, because it is in those moments that **his character shows through.** How you treat people who can do nothing for you is a sure sign of who you are. It's easy to say that a guy is nice to his friends because he knows them or to his family because they are, well, a family. And you could even say that he is trying to get his enemies to change and to like him when he loves them back. But when he is loving to a stranger, it's all about his character. People who are watching are intrigued, and the people who he loves are impressed. Loving people you don't know reminds you that we are all part of the same human race. It gives hope to miserable people and gives a little idea of the love of God to the world.

When a God Guy meets another human being, he sees not a stranger but another valuable soul. That means that he doesn't ignore the people around him as if they are just extras in the movie in which he is the star. He connects with them, even if that's just with eye contact and a smile. When he gets onto an elevator, he is friendly, even making small talk. When he sits next to someone in a theater, he says hello. When he is waited on by a server, he talks to him or her as a person and not as a servant. He takes a genuine interest in the souls around him whether they are beautiful or not. And because of that, he represents God well.

When a God Guy sees a stranger in need, he doesn't skip a beat; he helps them immediately. **He stands up for the weak and the ugly.** He makes the human race his family and the family of faith his brothers and sisters. If the God Guy doesn't care for the strangers God puts in his path, he runs the risk of missing out on the call on his life to love his neighbors as himself.

If you want to be a bridge to God for a dying world, then you have to open yourself up to show kindness and compassion to strangers. This is not just a good idea but a command: "Do not neglect to show hospitality to strangers, for by this some have entertained angels without knowing it" (Hebrews 13:2 NLT). **Be willing to trust God and step out,** even though you may fear others' response. This life isn't about how they respond but about how you respond to God's call to **love. Be brave, God Guy, and you will surely be rewarded!**

Let me tell you a story about a dad and his kid. When his dad left him—when his dad gave up on the family and went to live his own life—he had to make a choice. At first he hated. If his dad would give up on him, he would give up on his dad. But for some reason, one day he tried something new. He decided to **give love without**

expecting anything in return. And so he stopped hating and started loving. His dad didn't change. He didn't become a good guy all of a sudden, but something did change. They hung out. They did things. Sometimes his dad forgot and didn't show up, but he didn't let that change how he did his job of loving him. And suddenly he found that he actually felt okay about his dad. He had some moments with him that were good. And all the hate was gone. That gave him strength and the power to love not only his dad but others. This is a true story, except the kid in the story wasn't a he but a she. And that she is my wife Hayley. Unfortunately, this kind of story is all too common for both guys and girls.

If you let the hate of someone else become your hate, you lose. You give them the keys to your life and let them get into the driver's seat. You have to choose who will control you, man or God. Love is never a waste of your time or a bad choice. Love is an act of faith. And the Father returns love to anyone who is willing to receive it. "Because you love me, I will rescue you. I will protect you because you know my name" (Psalm 91:14).

Loving isn't just a suggestion; IT'S THE VERY COMMAND

on which all other commands are based.

Without love, we as believers have nothing. But take heart: love never fails. It might be rejected, it might give you pain, but that doesn't make it less valuable or rewarding to your soul. The God Guy will be known by his love. And the love that he offers will impact not only the hearts of those who receive it but the heart of the guy who gives it.

Double G Checklist

Here are a few practical ways to express what you've learned in this chapter. You don't have to do all of them, but you can. Just look at the list and see which things you think might help you know love.

> **Turning the other cheek**—This week do a study on humility. What is it? How did Jesus exemplify it? Find all the verses on it. Then apply them to your life. Learn how to be humble and to turn the other cheek no matter how crazy it seems. Either God's Word is true all the time or it's just plain wrong. If you believe it's right, then you've got to act on it no matter what the circumstance.

> **Love orphans and widows**—"*Pure, unstained religion, according to God our Father, is to take care of orphans and widows when they suffer and to remain uncorrupted by this world.*" (James 1:27) This week try to find a way to obey God's command to love. Offer to cut the lawn of the old woman down the street. Visit a sick person at the hospital.

Find a way to help those in need, like by getting donations or creating a clothes or food closet at your church for people in need. Take action, and show the world that God changes lives.

Your love list—If you are living on the dark side of life, turn things around by creating a list of everything you are thankful for. Write down the names of everyone you love and everything that shows you how much God loves you. Then find a way each day to show your appreciation for one person or thing in your life. For example, spend the day with your dad and talk about him, not you. Or to show you appreciate the roof over your head, clean up the house. Show your appreciation of God's expression of love to you by taking care of it.

God's love list—As a God Guy you have to know what pleases God so you can know what to do. So find out what pleases him. Then write it down. Get a blank journal that will be your "God Loves" list. Then make a list of things that God loves. He loves obedience, humility, kindness, peace, and so on. Write down all the verses you can find that apply to each thing that he loves. Over time, if you keep this up, you'll have a nice little book filled with all the things that will make the God you love happy. Well, *the book* won't make God happy but *you living it out* will make him rejoice. And every time you make God happy, you are sure to find peace and love for yourself.

3

A Guy Who Knows True Happiness

During the decade-plus when I was

FAKING MY FAITH,

I failed miserably at trying to look and act the part of a Christian while also trying to get whatever I wanted from the world. And the main thing I wanted was sex. I was **obsessed** with it. But once I got it, I felt like I had to be the good Christian guy and start down the road toward marriage, even though the more I found out about whichever girl I was dating, the more I became convinced we didn't belong together. I didn't know how to deal with my urges, and I didn't know how to deal with getting out of a relationship I shouldn't have been in. So I looked for a release, and that release was gambling. Poker, blackjack, craps. You name it. I felt like the weight of the world was on me and the only way I could hold it up was to "escape" through gambling. I couldn't

deal with going without sex or breaking up with someone. It wasn't until I lost my job and made myself such
a living disaster that I finally learned how to deal.

I was a believer when those urges and dead-end
escapes tried to control me. But I had yet to truly take
God's Word and call it mine; instead I served the god
of my feelings. If I felt it, it must be true. That was my
motto. But as I dug deeper into God's Word, I started
to find out the opposite was true. I had often heard
and even believed that worry was calling God a liar.
After all, he said he is in control and that he will never
leave us or forsake us. He said worry is sin. He said to
trust him. I knew all that, but it wasn't until I learned
the secret to true happiness that I took the step from
knowing to doing.

A guy who knows true happiness is a guy
who knows truth and loves it. Unhappiness comes
when you know the truth but you aren't so happy about
it and when you do things that disagree with what you
know to be right. When you really believe God wants
the best for you but you aren't strong enough to do what
you know you should, that's when life gets all messed up.
A God Guy knows true happiness because he isn't lying
to himself about truth, but he puts all his faith on the fact
that God is trustworthy. And because of that, he's going
to let 'er rip and put all his hope in him. True happiness
is within the reach of anyone who would risk taking God
at his Word and refusing to believe anything else, even
if he feels it deeply or hears it repeatedly.

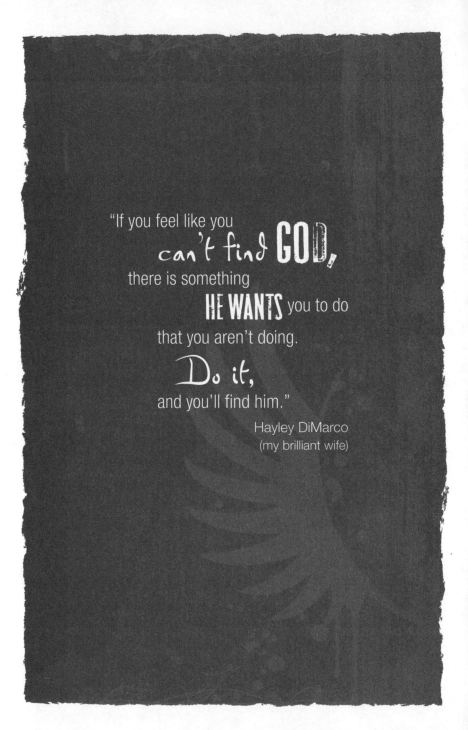

"If you feel like you **can't find GOD,** there is something **HE WANTS** you to do that you aren't doing. *Do it,* and you'll find him."

Hayley DiMarco
(my brilliant wife)

I don't believe that true happiness was meant to be an occasional thing or that life was meant to be empty or messy. But sometimes that's the case. Happy comes and happy goes. But true happiness is something different. It's an undying faith that no matter what happens, "it is well with my soul." It's a steady belief that God is not only all knowing but also all powerful, and because of that all of life has meaning, even the bad parts. True happiness isn't turning your back on the harsh realities of life. It isn't grinning in the face of heartache and loss. But it is a steady belief in the God who can overcome anything and because of that a firm belief that

"WITH GOD, I CAN! NO MATTER WHAT THE ODDS, I CAN!"

The God Guy may have the weight of the world on his shoulders, he might be in serious pain, but he never feels like his strength or life is in danger, because he knows he is protected. Someone else is bearing the weight. The God Guy knows that "He will cover you with his feathers, and under his wings you will find refuge. His truth is your shield and armor" (Psalm 91:4).

When your life is lacking true happiness, you can do something about it. Life doesn't have to stay the way it is; you can take charge if you are just willing to take God at his Word. So let's find out how you can bring true happiness to your life to stay.

Tell Yourself the Truth

The pursuit of truth is at the core of every God Guy. Knowing the truth, loving the truth, and determining to only think things that are true leads his to true happiness. That means that he doesn't let lies become a part of his vocabulary. "I can't." "I'm scared." "I'm too weak." "Life is too hard." These lies, these things that disagree with God, aren't good for your manhood. They give you the opposite of happiness. They breed despair and fear. God wants to give you more. He wants to give you the most that you could ever receive, and all you have to do is tell yourself the truth. And the only way to know what that truth is, is to look into the Word of God. In every area where he has trouble, the God Guy searches out the truth and then repeats it to himself. He takes those lies he's been believing and edits them out of his vocabulary. If you want to find true happiness, then take a look at the lies you believe. Here are just a few—do any of them sound familiar?

A God Guy doesn't let lies become a part of his vocabulary. "I can't." "I'm scared." "I'm too weak." "Life is too hard." These lies that disagree with God aren't good for your manhood.

Some lies guys believe:

God cannot forgive what I did.

My life would be better if _____ loved me.

God won't save me from what I fear the most.

No one believes in me, not even God.

I can't handle it when people don't like me.

Anytime you say "I can't," "It's too hard," "I'm depressed," or "I'm afraid"; anytime you panic or worry; anytime you act in anger, bitterness, or frustration— you are lying to yourself. You are saying something that flat out isn't true. I know that because these thoughts and the ones that lead to these conclusions disagree with what God says in his Word.

God's Word is all TRUE,

so if what you say or believe is the opposite of God's Word, it's a lie. Lies make you unhappy. They destroy lives and make things difficult. But the truth gives you strength, hope, and power. So take a look at the truth and see how much the lies get it wrong:

"I can't." "It's too hard." When these words have to do with obeying God's Word they are not true. God never commands you to do something impossible. In fact everything that he commands he will help you to do. That means it's all possible! All of it. "I can't" is a lie—if it's something God wants you to do then your only response is "I must."

"I'm depressed." A depressed mind is a mind focused on lies instead of truth. God's Word, the truth, was given in order to set you free. And knowing his Word and believing it will set you free from your occasional depression. God promises to give joy to those who love him; it is a fruit of the spirit given to those who remain connected to the vine (Galatians 5:22; Ecclesiastes 2:26). And it is a command: *"Always be joyful"* (1 Thessalonians 5:16). Since God never commands the impossible it must be so.

"I'm afraid." In the book of Jeremiah it says, "'Don't be afraid of people. I am with you, and I will rescue you,' declares the Lord" (Jeremiah 1:8). And in Psalms we read, "So we will not fear when earthquakes come and the mountains crumble into the sea" (Psalm 46:2). When you have fear in your life, go to God's Word and find hope and protection. You are protected by the Creator of the universe. What could harm you? Nothing, except that he allows it for your benefit. Like Joseph being thrown into jail you must know that God has everything under control and will work all things together for the good of those who love him (Romans 8:28).

All people have sinned, they have fallen short of God's glory. They receive God's approval freely by an act of his kindness through the price Christ Jesus paid to set

Any problem that comes between God and myself springs out of disobedience; any problem, and there are many, that is alongside me while I obey God, increases my ecstatic delight, because I know that my Father knows, and I am going to watch and see how He unravels this thing.

Oswald Chambers

us free [from sin]. God showed that Christ is the throne of mercy where God's approval is given through faith in Christ's blood.

Romans 3:23–25

I can do everything through Christ who strengthens me.

Philippians 4:13

He will put his angels in charge of you to protect you in all your ways.

Psalm 91:11

Never worry about anything. But in every situation let God know what you need in prayers and requests while giving thanks.

Philippians 4:6

Blessed are you when people insult you, persecute you, lie, and say all kinds of evil things about you because of me.

Matthew 5:11

Take Every Thought Captive

Finally, brothers and sisters, keep your thoughts on whatever is right or deserves praise: things that are true, honorable, fair, pure, acceptable, or commendable.

Philippians 4:8

Happiness is always just a thought away. Think weak thoughts and you'll be weak; think successful thoughts and you'll be successful. That's why God calls you to think about the good things in life, not the bad stuff. The truth is that it isn't what happens to you that makes you miserable but what you think about what happens to you that controls your emotions. Your happiness is under your own control. When you refuse to concentrate on the negative parts of life, you take those negative thoughts captive (see 2 Corinthians 10:5). Then all that is left is to replace those thoughts with things that are true, good, praiseworthy, and honorable.

Think about it like this: you get whatever you plant. When you plant a tomato seed in the ground, you don't expect to get a crop of potatoes. The same is true of your mind: when you fill it with seeds of negative thinking, complaining, and worrying, you get negative feelings, depression, anger, and bitterness. But when you plant seeds of hope and faith, you get good feelings—feelings of hope, faith, life, and happiness. Your garden is yours to till and to plant. What kind of crops do you want to harvest? Choose that, and then get to work with the seeds of that crop.

So how do you take thoughts captive? It takes two things. The first is you have to know

YOU ARE
What You *Think*

"Man is chained only by himself. Thoughts are the jailers
of Fate—they imprison, being
base; they are also the angels of Freedom—they liber-
ate, being noble. Not what he
wished and prays for does a
man get, but what he har-
bors within. His wishes and
prayers are only gratified and
answered when they harmo-
nize with his thoughts."

James Allen,
As a Man Thinketh

the law. A cop can't be a good cop if he doesn't know the law. He can't arrest people unless he knows that what they are doing is illegal. The same goes for your thoughts. You've got to know what is acceptable and what isn't. So learn God's Word. Find out what he wants from you, and when your mind wanders off into unlawful subjects, grab those thoughts, throw them out the door, and slam it shut. Then turn around and think about something that is lawful. Replace those wrong thoughts with truth. You have to stop the bad thoughts as soon as you notice them, and each time you do that, you'll notice them earlier and earlier. You can't let them become a habit. Refuse them each time they pop up, and you'll start to gain more and more control of your own mind.

The God Guy tells himself the truth even when everything in him argues against it. Learn the truth. Make it your weapon against failure and self-destruction. Don't ever let how you feel dictate what you believe. Feelings lie, but God's Word never does.

THE GOD GUY tells himself the truth

63

Agree with God

The quickest way to happiness is to agree with God, because when you disagree with him, finding the strength to do what's right is difficult. "No one can please God without faith" (Hebrews 11:6). Can you agree that all of God's Word is good and the best choice for your life? If you can't, then you are gonna lose out on true happiness. Disagreeing with God's commands can bring instant satisfaction, but over time the result of disagreeing with him and his call on your life will be emotional, spiritual, and maybe even physical pain.

Wanna test your thoughts? Think about it like this: any thought that disagrees with God is a lie, because God speaks only truth.

"He is a **ROCK.** What he does is *perfect.* All his ways are *fair.* He is a **FAITHFUL GOD,** who does no wrong. He is **HONORABLE and RELIABLE**" (Deuteronomy 32:4).

When you lie to yourself, you sin. And sin leads you away from true happiness. Worry calls God a liar and leads to emotional and physical trauma, ulcers, panic attacks, isolation, and the list goes on. Fear rejects God's truth and leads to depression, paranoia, failure, and

64

DISAGREEMENT

Here are some ways that you disagree with God.
You disagree with him when you

- doubt
- fear
- worry
- hate
- fight back
- lust
- lose control
- get impatient
- hold a grudge
- get revenge
- resent
- get depressed
- hurt yourself
- hurt others
- obsess over
  something
- overindulge
- or refuse to help.

much more. Stress says God won't do what God says he will do. But you can't know what that is if you don't know God's Word. So in order to agree with him, you have to hear him out. You want more strength, more control? Then you've gotta get into God's Word and find out what he's thinking.

Every time you disagree with God and his Word, you hurt yourself and your relationship with God. If you want true happiness, the kind that never leaves, then you've gotta agree with God on every point and refuse to be bullied by any other thoughts. And God is gonna give you a man-sized portion of happiness (see Ecclesiastes 2:26).

Get Over It

> Though your sins are bright red, they will become as white as snow. Though they are dark red, they will become as white as wool.
>
> Isaiah 1:18

The God Guy is a guy who doesn't hold on to failure or mess-ups. He believes the Bible when it says that "God is faithful and reliable. If we confess our sins, he forgives them and cleanses us from everything we've done wrong" (1 John 1:9). So the God Guy doesn't hold on to the past, holding himself hostage to his mistakes. Instead he accepts forgiveness and so refuses to rehash his sin, to punish himself, or to define himself by what he did in the past. Forgiveness is freedom for the God Guy. It gives him a clean slate. It cleanses him and makes him white as snow.

To refuse forgiveness is to argue with God. If you've done something wrong, you can't hang on to it as if you are a particularly hard case, someone too bad for God to forgive. Remember, if Christ's death on the cross isn't enough to forgive your sins, then Christ died for nothing (see Galatians 2:21). Your sin is never a shock to God, and you are never so bad that he won't take you back.

You have to get over the bad stuff of the past, your sin, and even the sins of others. When you hold on to it, you just torture yourself. When you refuse to get over things, you hold on to sin as if it is your salvation, your only hope, but that is a lie. Letting go is where your strength lies. So refuse to hold on to anything—any memory, any worry, or any fear—that comes from sin.

That means that if you are holding a grudge, you've got to let go of it. Holding on to it is a sin. It's not taking a position of power; it's sin, and so it's weakness. So right now, this minute, get over it! If you think getting even with someone is your job, then you've lost your way. Who do you think you are—God? "'Vengeance is Mine, I will repay,' says the Lord" (Hebrews 10:30 NKJV). Don't get even. Don't sit around plotting and planning. Get over it. If there is something you can't get over, then you've got a big weakness that is going to tear you down eventually.

Trash Your Idols

An idol is anything that you are obsessed with and can't get out of your mind. Idols aren't just little wooden figurines or golden cows; they are preoccupations of the mind, things you believe will make you happy or relieve your pain or fear. An idol tries to take the place of God by offering you some kind of hope.

I used to have one—well, a few actually, but the worst was sugar. Whenever I got bummed or just worn out I would go on a sugar binge and it would lift my spirits. Give me relief. But then it wanted more and more of me. Hey, it even *became* more and more of me via weight gain. Sugar became my idol at the point that I couldn't control it any-more. I had to demolish the Golden Donut.

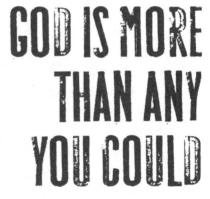

Idols will run your life and steal your happiness. At first they promise great stuff, but then they start to control you, to talk to you, to promise you things they can never truly give. If you have anything in your life that you are obsessed with, then you have idol trouble. Is there anything that if I asked you right now to give up, you couldn't? Then you have an idol.

Idols are bad for you. They offer a false happiness and have to be trashed in order to get to true happiness. If you want freedom from the things that seem to control you, then you are in luck. All you need to do is to call them what they are, false gods, and then refuse to worship them. That means get them out of your life. Take away their altars. If it's a video game that obsesses you, get rid of your XBox and stop talking about it. If it's cars, refuse to let them be all you think about and talk about.

Whatever you do that you hate, that you want to stop but can't seem to, is an idol. Know that God hates it too, and because of that he is by your side to help you kick it out. And remember, he is more powerful than any other god you could find. But he won't ever do it by himself—he wants you to agree with him and to call your idol an idol. You have the power to be idol free; you just have to own it and then use it. When you do, you will find an ton of true happiness.

POWERFUL OTHER GOD FIND.

Live a Life of Contentment

The God Guy finds happiness by living a life of contentment. To be content is to be happy with what you have and even with what you don't have. When you tell yourself that you should have something you don't have or that what you have is bad, you are discontent.

God in Mind

You are the branch and he is the vine. When water, sunlight, and nutrients cover the soil, they are drawn up through the vine and into the branches. When you give God the glory as you do things for him, in a weird way it feeds you as well. Doing things with God in mind and for his good will always give you the most strength and nourishment. If it is through the vine that you are fed, then why wouldn't you give everything you have to the vine?

It isn't easy to be content; it takes work, and it can feel like you are lying to yourself. After all, how can you say you are content when what you have isn't enough or isn't what you imagined? It's a hard question and one that most people would ask.

Finding happy can't depend on things, because when it does those things disappoint or disappear. Sure, happiness can come from stuff. I know that a new Xbox game can bring me joy for days. But it eventually loses its cool factor, and my happiness meter drops. When you put your hope for happiness any place but in the **hands of God**, you not only are out for failure, but you make bad and even hurtful decisions.

Look at the effects of divorce on kids across the world. When a person decides that a marriage is responsible for their happiness or lack thereof and so walks away when things get tough, they can bring pain to more than just themselves. To this I can attest. I've seen the search for happiness in the eyes of another destroy many a family. I've seen what it did to my wife's family. And I confess I've done the same thing. I've hurt many a heart over my belief that a particular girl would bring me joy.

THE MIND OF A GOD GUY ISN'T SET ON FINDING HAPPINESS ONLY IN THE WORLD;

he holds a firm belief that an unmoving true happiness can be found not here on earth but in the eyes of his Fa-

> WHEN YOU ARE WILLING TO PUT PLEASING HIM ABOVE EVERYTHING ELSE—EVEN ABOVE PLEASING YOURSELF—YOU WILL FIND THE SECRET TO TRUE HAPPINESS.

ther. When you are willing to put pleasing him above everything else—even above pleasing yourself—you will find the secret to true happiness.

Contentment isn't based on what you have but on who you know. The apostle Paul says that he learned the secret of contentment, whether he had stuff or had nothing, and the secret was that he could do everything through the one who gave him strength (see Philippians 4:13). That one is Jesus. That means that contentment says, "I don't need this or that to do what needs to be done." And it definitely doesn't need anything other than Christ himself to be happy. When Christ becomes all you need, you will find happiness all around you, because he never disappoints.

Here are some ways you can practice contentment:

1. **Prioritize.** Determine that your biggest goal should be storing up treasure in heaven, not here on earth (see Matthew 6:20–21). Look at your priorities and connect them to your treasures. Where is what you gain or give with each

priority storing up your treasures? If you don't like where your storehouse is located do something about reprioritizing.

2. **Simplify.** Find contentment and happiness in learning to live with less (see Matthew 8:20; Acts 4:32).

3. **Help others.** Knowing that contentment for the God Guy comes from pleasing God, find contentment by getting outside yourself and helping those in need (see Proverbs 21:13; 1 John 3:17).

4. **Learn to enjoy what you do have.** Use it, love it, share it (see 1 Timothy 6:8).

Find Happiness on the Other Side of Heartache

As a God Guy you don't have to be happy all the time. You are a real human being with real feelings and real circumstances that will lead to grief and sadness, good times and bad. And none of that is wrong. In fact, the apostle Paul tells us to "Be happy with those who are happy. Be sad with those who are sad" (Romans 12:15). There is room in the life of a God Guy to feel more than just happiness. But happiness is generally the preferred emotion. And when things get painful and hard to handle, happiness is always that thing that you wish you could find.

Shortly after high school I was neck deep in a relationship with a girl I knew for sure that I was going to

73

marry. We were involved in church, she was in school at our hometown university, and I was taking a break from school and working, trying to figure out what to do next. The one thing I didn't need to figure out was my relationship. I was in it to win it. Even when she decided to move out of state to finish her degree, I was committed to making it work. To show her my dedication, I drove ten hours to surprise her on Valentine's Day. She was blown away when I showed up at her new job with roses in hand and was excited to introduce me to her aunt and uncle she was living with while she established residency in that state.

But what I didn't know was that since I was so focused on the relationship and not my academics or future career, I think I freaked my girlfriend's parents out just a tad. Ok, more than a tad. I freaked them out to the point that they bribed their daughter to move out of state and enroll in a much more expensive school just to get her away from me! In fact, when my girlfriend's parents found out from her aunt that I was getting ready to sleep on their couch for the night, the aunt handed me the phone and her parents told me I wasn't any good for their daughter and I wasn't allowed to stay there. With no money and my face drenched in tears, I slept in my car outside the aunt and uncle's home crushed that her parents didn't think I measured up, and pulverized that my girlfriend chose her parents and a fancy school over me.

It still pains me to this day, but not in the same way. It pains me that her parents were right.

I wasn't ready and I was potentially stopping their daughter from realizing her goals. Even more, while God was clearly calling me to be used by him, I ran from that heartache in the opposite direction away from him. I think it was A. W. Tozer that said, "God does not use someone greatly until he hurts them deeply." When pain comes at you from outside of yourself (in other words, when it isn't self-inflicted), you can be sure that God wants to use it to make you stronger and more devoted. But he can't do that if you aren't willing to see the strength in it, the power to turn away from introspection and to God's Word and truth. Happiness comes after the pain, when you allow pain to do its work. No one can find happiness in the hard times better than a God Guy, because

HAPPINESS depends on knowing God's hand is at work NO MATTER WHAT THE CIRCUMSTANCE (see Romans 8:28).

When I'm at the end of my rope and have lost all patience and hope, I find a quiet room and drop to my knees. I usually pray sitting, but in these moments, I kneel down and bury my face into the carpet. And I get real with God. Instead of starting with how much I adore him, I start with how messed up things feel and

God who COMFORTS

how messed up I feel. Then I shut up and listen. I wait for him to come and be God to me—he who comforts and counsels me (see Isaiah 9:6; 2 Corinthians 1:4).

I know that when I have a willing mind and heart, God will come to me and remind me of something in his Word, something that I've forgotten or ignored that I know to be true. That's why it's so important to open the Bible and just read even when you don't feel like it. The books I read when I'm least inspired are Proverbs and Philippians. Proverbs gives easy-to-understand nuggets of wisdom, and Philippians really hits home about how we should consider God (above all) and consider others (better than ourselves.) Then there's always Psalms. Psalms reminds me that I can trust that he will not leave me in my misery. Instead, he will point out to me where I am seeing the world with human eyes instead of godly eyes. He shows me the most important things, like learning to love others, even the irritating ones, and learning to live on the love of God alone and no one else. He is truly all you need, my brother.

If you are broken down and hurting all over, you have someone who never disappoints and never leaves you.

You've gotta find a way to get to him. Talk to him, but also remember to listen. His way of thinking is different from the world's. He will never talk to you about what you deserve and should have but will tell you what you don't need to worry about or fear. Happiness comes when you turn your eyes away from your needs and onto your God. When your needs become your focus, you are gonna find sadness, because in this world you will never get everything you want. Jesus confirmed it when he said, "I've told you this so that my peace will be with you. In the world you'll have trouble. But cheer up! I have overcome the world" (John 16:33). You can trust his words. You can trust that he has something greater for you than you are worried about right now, and if you are just willing to look into his eyes and believe him, he will show it all to you.

Your life is full of possibilities. Even in pain and heartache, your life can get better. Some of the most amazing people in the world are people who went through great pressure and heartache. Look at Lance Armstrong and what he did *after* he was diagnosed with an often fatal form of cancer. He only won a jil-

God who COUNSELS

lion Frenchy bike races over insane elevations. When you refuse to let circumstance dictate who you are and what you will achieve, you can ride over the mountains of monotony, isolation, pain, and even disaster to great heights of success and faith.

True happiness is within your reach.

You do not need to live in weakness and fear. The life of the God Guy is one of complete trust in the words of God. He knows that all things "work together for the good of those who love God—those whom he has called according to his plan" (Romans 8:28). And because of that the God Guy is fearless and full of hope. Hope produces true happiness because hope believes anything is possible. Hope doesn't despair; it doesn't doubt; it believes. Trust God with your life and trust his Word, and you will have more happy than you know what to do with.

> I am convinced that nothing can ever separate us from God's love which Christ Jesus our Lord shows us. We can't be separated by death or life, by angels or rulers, by anything in the present or anything in the future, by forces or powers in the world above or in the world below, or by anything else in creation.
>
> Romans 8:38–39

Double G Checklist

My obsessions—What are you obsessed with? Think about it. What do you spend most of your time thinking about? Is it affecting your emotions? Your relationships? Your spirit? If you don't like what your thoughts are doing to you, then this week make a change. Note all of your obsessions and make a plan for getting rid of them. Obsessed with your computer? Cut down your time on it to one hour per day. Obsessed with girls? Fill your free time with your bros and time studying the Word. Make it impossible to obsess about anything other than God.

Getting over it—Are there some things in your past you just haven't gotten over? What are they? Try this. This week spend some time in worship. Tell God how great he is. Adore him. Then ask him to point out the things you aren't willing to let go of but need to. As things come to mind, write them down. Then tell God thank you for his forgiveness and tell him you agree with him that what is done is done. Refuse to sin longer by holding on to your sin. Once you have a list of things, or even just one, write a prayer. Confess how you have gone wrong by holding on to your sin. Promise to let go. And express your belief that God is big enough to take the stain of it away. He might not remove the consequences, but you can thank him for them because they taught you what was wrong. Don't allow anything to be used for bad, but let it be used only for good.

Toss your thoughts—When Hayley and I were dating, she was still dealing with a lot of stress, fear, and worry. One day I took her to the river and handed her a bag of rocks. On each rock I had written one of her sins—worry, fear, and so on. I told her to take each one, say the sin out loud, repent from it, and then to throw the rock into the water. For her it was a powerful visual of God's power to remove her sin from her as far as the east is from the west. Throwing it into the depths of the water never to be seen again gave her strength and reminded her that she was in control of her thoughts and not the world or the circumstances that surrounded her. So if you are willing, try this experience yourself. No river nearby? Go to a cliff and throw them off. Or write them on paper and burn it in a bucket or push it through a shredder. Just create a symbol of getting rid of the things that you think often that call God a liar.

Simplify—Wanna practice not loving things of this world? Then give simplicity a try. Go through your stuff and give away, sell, or trash ten things. If there is something you cannot let go of, ask yourself, "Why? What does it mean to me?" Simplicity helps you keep the main thing the main thing and make "things" unimportant. Do some research on simplicity and give it a chance.

4

A Guy Who Knows
How to
Communicate

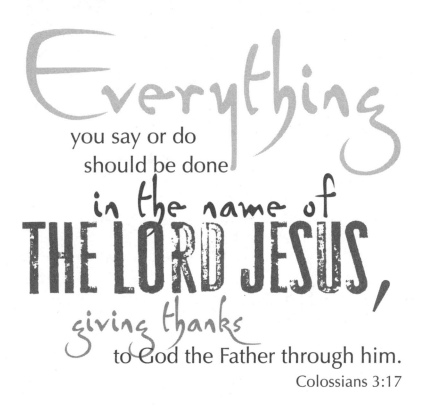

Everything you say or do should be done in the name of THE LORD JESUS, giving thanks to God the Father through him.

Colossians 3:17

I don't know about you, but I love cracking a joke. My dear old dad was a joke teller—funny stories with a long setup. But I'm more of a quick wit guy. The zinger, the play on words. It's pretty gratifying to make someone laugh, whether it's to build on new friendships or make new ones.

But I took it to extremes in my younger days. Sometimes I just wouldn't know when to stop, like when I'd get in trouble for "disrupting the class" or started to make my way into the working world. Worse yet, I was a big sarcasm guy. I thought that if it was truly funny, it couldn't be wrong, because hey, it was funny! It was nothing personal; it was strictly business. Funny business! I thought people who couldn't take a joke had a thin skin and needed to get over it. I would even drop an F-bomb here and there just for the shock factor. Before long, I had one group of friends I could use a cuss word in every single sentence with and another group where we'd sing "Kumbayah." I was leading a double life again—no true me, no true character.

After I got to know Jesus and his character and love, my communication style changed. My jokes were still quick-witted, but I wasn't as gross, lewd, or mean. My jokes were less about other people and more about harmless funny. No more fat jokes. The other big thing was dropping the dripping sarcasm. That habit was hard to break, but it helped that a song lyric got stuck in my head about someone who felt taller by making other people smaller.

I finally decided that the life I led in front of my old drinking buddies was going to be the same as the one in front of my church men's group buddies. That meant that I had to stop cussing and sharing dirty jokes with my non-Christian homies. And an amazing thing happened. I didn't give some "I'm holier now" speech; I just stopped. When they started to tell a joke that was out of bounds, I didn't say, "WHOA THERE!" I just quickly changed the subject or coincidentally had to go to the bathroom. So what was the amazing thing? They almost stopped the cussing and dirty joke telling around me. Sure, they slipped up now and then, but we're talking a 90 percent reduction at least. Why is that, do you think? My guess is that when your life and your way of communicating is more like Jesus—when your words and attitude have changed how you treat people—it can have a huge effect on the lives of others around you.

The God Guy is oftentimes the only Bible that others will read. And that means that as a God Guy, you must

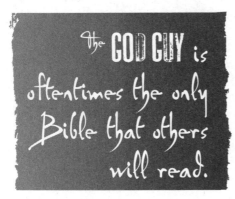

be aware that what you say, how you talk, and how you communicate with others can affect the eternity of the people around you. As a God Guy your speech and ways of communicating reflect the character of God. When you are kind, compassionate, and a good listener, people catch a glimpse of the heavenly, and it can give them hope. You should never underestimate your impact on the world. The God Guy knows the world is watching—and they aren't watching him but Christ in him—so he works hard to communicate the love and grace of the Christ who first loved him.

Being a God Guy means being aware of what your words and actions are saying about your God. So let's look at some ways you can communicate his love.

Show Kindness

Kindness isn't weakness; it's charming. It draws others in and makes them feel safe. Kindness might seem like an unmanly trait, but that would be a lie. Kindness is a man's way of sharing God with the world. When people who are serving me are short with me (not height-wise), angry, or just disinterested, I always try to be extra nice and bring them out of their shell. I try to get into their world, stop their cycle of "whatever," and bring a smile to their day. It isn't much, but it is a taste of the kindness and love of Christ, and it might change their entire day. In fact, in some cases, one act of kindness could save their entire life. You can never underestimate the value of kindness, and for a Double G, anything less is unacceptable. God's kindness to you is your inspiration and your model for your kindness to the world. Kindness is a simple expression of love that opens up a world of possibilities.

Being kind isn't always easy, though. Mean people, grumpy people, busy people don't make it easy. Kindness isn't always the easiest response to those types of people, but it needs to be our response (see Psalm 39:1). In my younger days I got

KINDNESS isn't always the EASIEST RESPONSE but it needs to be our response.

way beyond serious with a girl I dated. This was before I knew what true faith in God was and in the beginning days of me being a fake—you know, living two different ways depending on the people around me. Needless to say, living that way can hurt a lot of people, and I hurt this girl emotionally. I asked for forgiveness and thought I had gotten it, but every so often I get a nasty email or an "anonymous" comment on the Web from her.

Trust me, I want to go off on her—tell her all the ways she messed up, how she hurt me too, and how what she's doing is wack. But I don't. I've had to learn to be kind. When she's civil, I repay that with kindness. When she's a jerk (a lady jerk), I am kind and say, "I'm sorry you're still hurt by that, but I wish you the best," and leave it at that. I really think she wants me to go off on her so she can prove I'm the same as I was, because then she doesn't have to let go of the hurt or deal with the thought that I'm a better person now. The fact is, I'm not a better person, I just have a better Person controlling my life. A kind and merciful God dwelling inside me. Kindness not only draws out the kindness of others but also reminds them of their meanness;

it convicts them. Refusing to be kind never achieves good results. It only makes things worse. Sure, it feels good to retaliate or to ignore someone, but the end result isn't good (see Proverbs 15:1).

The God Guy makes every effort to be kind to everyone, no matter who they are or what they can or can't do for him (see Proverbs 17:27). Kindness is his gift to a busy and stressed out world. Here are some practical ways to practice kindness every day:

1. **Smile at people.** A smile can change a person's day and make them feel connected. When you don't smile, people can assume you are insecure or arrogant, even though you may just be thinking about something else. So do your best to smile at people that you meet, walk past, or look at.

2. **Look them in the eyes.** Looking people in the eyes is not only kind, but it's also confident. It says to them, "You count." And it reminds them that we are all part of the same human race. When you avoid looking people in the eyes, you seem cold and unattached, and that doesn't help to spread the love of Christ but hides it.

3. **Offer a hand.** When someone is struggling with something heavy, offer them a hand. When someone looks lost, ask them if you can help. What guy doesn't want to be a hero? When you offer to help people, you share kindness with them and lighten their load.

4. **Say hello.** In today's busy world it's easy to become isolated from others, oblivious to the pain and concern of the people around us. But kindness gets involved; it steps into the lives of others, even if only to say hi. Say hi to anyone who looks you in the eyes. Say hi to people who wait on you or serve you in any way. Even if they don't look at you, interrupt their isolation and say hello. When you do, you look like a strong and confident guy.

5. **Give.** Kindness gives to people in need. I can remember when I saw a woman in front of me in line who couldn't buy everything she had in her cart and was putting something back. I said, "Here, I can cover it." I handed a couple of bucks to the clerk and paid for her stuff. Kindness finds a need and helps where it can.

Put Others First

The backbone of the God Guy is that he isn't about "me" all the time. He lives outside of himself. He sees other people and takes notice of their pain, their joy, their fear. He is forever thinking from an eternal perspective and is confident enough in his relationship with Christ to know that **life is not about him** but about loving others so that they might know Christ as he does.

That's why in all his speech, he puts others first. He doesn't monopolize conversations, insisting others hear all about his feelings and thoughts. But he asks a lot of questions and listens to the answers. He draws people out. He doesn't talk to be heard or to feel better. And he knows that if what he has to say is only to make himself feel good, then it's best if it's not said. He isn't self-seeking and doesn't need the approval of others to be secure, so he takes his baggage and his stuff to his God and lets others be free from the burden. That means that talking with him is easy. He doesn't always turn the conversation back to himself, and he responds to what people are saying with more than an "Oh," or "I see." He makes conversation about things that interest the people he is talking to. Talking has become a selfish activity for many, but for the God Guy it is an opportunity to give others the gift of human interaction and support.

When in doubt, TALK.

The biggest trap for a lot of guys when it comes to communication is that we don't talk. People need us to talk in order to be heard. So even if you don't have anything to say, ask questions and show you are listening by agreeing with what the person is saying or encouraging them to tell you more. And in all your speech, always be thinking of *balance*. Listen well but also be willing to share yourself a little.

If you find it hard to talk much, then open up the ears and think about trying some of these things next time you're going to hang out with someone:

1. **Pray for them.** Before you meet up with someone, pray for them. Praying for them gets your mind on the big picture and off of yourself.
2. **Get some questions.** Before you go, think of at least five things you want to ask the person about themselves. Like an interviewer interviewing a famous person, take some time to think about what you

could ask them that would start a good conversation about them.

3. **Praise them.** Try to find at least two things about them to praise. When you are looking for the good in them, you won't be thinking about yourself as much.

Respects Authority

Anyone who rebels against authority is rebelling against what God has instituted, and they will be punished.

Romans 13:2 NLT

The God Guy understands that anyone who has authority over him must be respected. For a lot of us it's easier to respect friends and acquaintances than it is to respect people in authority over us, and that's probably because they are telling us what to do. But parents, bosses, teachers, police—anyone in authority is to be respected even though they are telling you to do something you hate. Respect, according to Romans 13:2 isn't based on how you feel about the person making demands, but their position of God given authority in your life.

Because of this, the God Guy is respectful of those in authority. Other people are always watching the God Guy to see if he is truly who he says he is, and a lack of respect for authority betrays a sinful heart that only confirms that his faith isn't changing him or making him more holy.

OBEDIENCE

to human beings isn't always easy.

They are imperfect, they may say things wrong, they may get things wrong, but that doesn't excuse disrespect. Your life can't be controlled by others' imperfections but should be ruled by God's perfection. That means you have to always act out of love for him, not reaction to them.

When a guy respects authority he stands tall, he is confident, he looks others in the eye, he promptly agrees to do what is asked, and he shows a level of honor and a fear of God that makes him easy to work with and live with. When you respect those in authority, you respect the God who put them there. Don't ever let bad authority figures be an excuse for your bad behavior, but prove yourself good and true by being obedient and respectful.

In order to respect authority:

1. **Don't argue.** When you argue with authority, you refuse authority. Bite your tongue and obey God.
2. **Don't roll your eyes when you disagree.** It's okay to disagree with authority in your mind, but you

can't be disrespectful by making your disagreement known, unless you do it in a respectful and
godly way.

3. **Don't mock them when they aren't around.** Others are around and they are listening, so don't
show them how to dishonor authority by complaining or mocking it.

4. **Don't ignore them.** When someone in authority
asks you to do something or even just talks to
you, never ignore them. It is disrespectful and
only makes the person who ultimately has control
over you angry. Not a good situation.

Listen

I have a friend who loves to talk. He talks and talks
and tells me everything about his life. Then when I
get a chance to tell him something about my life, he
listens, but as soon as I am done with a few sentences
he changes the subject back to him. And it's stupid.
Yeah, I said it.

Listening is more than being quiet while someone
talks. It is a gift of communication that you give to
people you care about.

Listening is actually hearing what the person says and responding to it in a way that
makes them feel heard and understood.

A God Guy knows that listening is required in order for there to be bonding and a personal connection. Two people can never truly know each other if one or both refuse to listen. For the longest time this friend of mine didn't even know what I did for a living. Can you imagine talking to someone for months on end without ever even knowing anything about them? It's not that unusual, but it shouldn't be like that in the life of the God Guy.

When people talk, make the effort to stop thinking about yourself and start thinking about them.

HERE'S HOW TO BE A good listener:

1. **Try to comment on what they are saying.** Don't let them say something without saying at least, "I know what you mean," or "That's too bad." Let them know you are listening by saying something that confirms it.

2. **Focus on them.** The worst thing is to talk to someone who is looking around the room, reading a book, or watching TV. Try giving people your undivided attention. Then they will know they are being heard.

Don't Make Stuff Up

Respect and admiration are two things that guys really want. So if you don't get any respect, sometimes it's easy to just make stuff up that will impress people. But making stuff up is a really weak way to get attention. I know—I was the king. And I hate to write this, but I learned it from my someone in my family. They'd even lie about stupid stuff, like if you asked, "Did you see *Seinfeld* this week?" They'd say, "Oh yeah, that was great!" and then not know anything about the show. It took me forever to unlearn this and change what I'd picked up from my family tree.

Do you really want people to appreciate and respect what you wish you were instead of who you really are? When you exaggerate, even just a little, you deceive people. And deception isn't cool. It definitely doesn't make you more of a man. And the truth is that your lies always get found out, and when they do you're gonna look worse than you would have if you'd never said anything.

The God Guy isn't afraid to be who he is without any additions to the truth.

THE GOD GUY ISN'T AFRAID TO BE WHO HE IS WITHOUT ANY ADDITIONS TO THE TRUTH.

If who he is does not live up to what others expect, he knows the problem is with their image of him and they have to deal with that.

Know When to Share Emotions

Girls and emotions seem to go hand-in-hand. Girls know their feelings and how to share them, but for guys it's not always that easy. Emotions can be hard to figure out, and knowing how much to share can be even harder. Most guys find it easiest to just keep their feelings under wraps. But some have learned to just let them flow and make other people figure out how to deal with them. Neither extreme is the best. The God Guy's emotional life is balanced. He knows when to share his emotions and when to keep them to himself.

One guideline to consider is this: never dump on a girl or a nonbeliever. When you share your rawest emotions with a girl, you have extreme intimacy on your hands. And with extreme intimacy before mar-

The God Guy's emotional life is balanced. He knows when to share his emotions and when to keep them to himself.

riage comes danger. The other thing dumping on a girl does is make you become "one of the girls." Kiss dating that girl good-bye unless she's wanting to lead the relationship. The reason you don't want to dump all your emotions on a nonbeliever is they aren't going to give you biblical advice. So basically you're either leaving yourself open to taking unwise counsel or you're in essence saying, **"I respect you enough to dump my emotions on you right now but not enough to take your advice,"** and that's insulting. So look for a **mature believer** who knows you and God well enough to speak truth into your life. But if all you seem to be doing on a weekly basis is looking for someone to dump on, watch out! "[Like] a city broken into [and] left without a wall, [so] is a person who lacks self-control" (Proverbs 25:28).

This doesn't mean you can't share your emotions. It just means that you choose to do it after you've considered both the need for those emotions to be shared and the impact of sharing them. Because guys can compartmentalize and separate different parts of their lives so well, it is easy to stand back and take a look at a situation before expressing emotion. So when you have an opportunity to say something that would tell people what you are feeling, consider a few things:

1. Will the sharing of this emotion hurt this person or make their life more miserable?

2. Will the sharing of this emotion make their life better?
3. Why do you want to tell them how you feel? Is it for their benefit or your own?
4. If you are having a hard time sharing your emotion, what do you fear about sharing how you feel?
5. Is what you fear impeding your ability to love this person?
6. What does God's Word say about this particular emotion and how it should be shared?

The answer to all these should always be *selfless,* focused on what is best for the other person. A lot of times people share just in order to get something off their chest or to feel better about themselves, but both of these are selfish and can oftentimes only hurt the person they are talking to. If what you want to say isn't going to improve the life of the person you are talking to, then stop and ask yourself, "Do I really need to say this?"

Don't Pick On the Weak

The God Guy is a protector of the weak. He believes God's Word that the meek will inherit the earth (see Matthew 5:5). He knows what an awful thing it is to put a stumbling block in front of a weaker brother (see Matthew 18:6). And so he is always aware of doing anything that might hurt another person. Actions have

"*Before,* you used
to go to this person and that,
but now the notion of the

DIVINE CONTROL

is forming so powerfully in you
that you go to God
about it."

Oswald Chambers

spiritual ramifications for the God Guy, so he makes all his decisions based on that instead of what he feels or what he wants.

The God Guy doesn't bully. It doesn't make you look good when you prove yourself more powerful than a weaker person. In fact, that's not true power at all. True spiritual power comes when you control your emotions and you reach out to help a weaker person instead of doing the obvious and stepping all over them. People of good character notice when other people are noble and courageous. Only those who are weak in character will applaud a guy who picks on a weaker person.

Don't Judge Others

As a person who knows God and his Word, you can find it very easy to judge others based on that knowledge. But to judge is to play God. You must judge for yourself what is good and what is sinful, but you cannot insult others for their actions. The God Guy doesn't say things in order to convict others but in order to love them. Conviction is God's job. The God Guy is never holier-than-thou; instead he is humble and thinks more highly of others than of himself. This entices people to know more about him and his God. Respect and an understanding that we all have sinned does more to draw people to the truth of God than a critical spirit ever could. God's Word makes it clear:

Connect the Branches

No branch is connected to another branch, except through the vine. So when you want to communicate with another branch, where you get in trouble is when you try to communicate branch-to-branch instead of going through the vine. That means that you have to communicate through Christ to reach another person. In other words, communicate in a Christlike manner. That means saying things without your own self-interest at heart and saying them in love.

When you look at a vine with many branches, you don't see the vine right away; you see all the branches. That's why it's doubly important that you represent the vine and draw in people who aren't a part of the vine, those branches scattered on the ground, through how you communicate. When a nonbeliever first sees you, they don't necessarily see you as a part of the entire plant, branches and vine. If you communicate in a godly way, you draw them closer to the vine, where God can graft them back into the vine. If a nonbeliever doesn't like the way you communicate, what then is going to attract them to the vine?

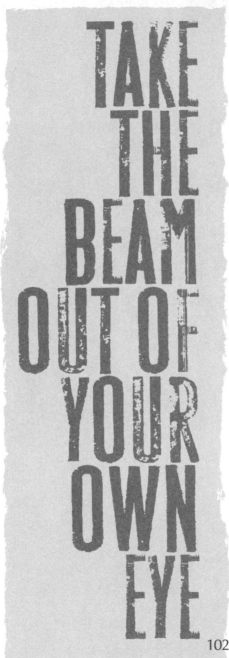

TAKE THE BEAM OUT OF YOUR OWN EYE

Stop judging so that you will not be judged. Otherwise, you will be judged by the same standard you use to judge others. The standards you use for others will be applied to you. So why do you see the piece of sawdust in another believer's eye and not notice the wooden beam in your own eye? How can you say to another believer, "Let me take the piece of sawdust out of your eye," when you have a beam in your own eye? You hypocrite! First remove the beam from your own eye. Then you will see clearly to remove the piece of sawdust from another believer's eye.

Matthew 7:1–5

Here are some things to put in your noggin when it comes to avoiding judging:

1. **Be Switzerland.** In the competition of life, choose to be neutral. Trust God to fight for you and protect you, and don't fight with others over their mistakes or problems. Also carry around a lot of chocolate.

2. **Don't think too highly of yourself because of your successes.** It's easy to judge others who don't have it together as much you do. Everything you have is a gift from God, so don't become proud when you look at others who don't have as much.

3. **Never compare yourself with others unless you are trying to make them look good.** It's easy to judge others when you compare their lives to yours, so avoid it.

4. **Don't be offended.** It's easy to judge others when what they do or say offends you. But as a believer you don't have the right to be offended. Jesus is your model, and he was never offended for himself—only for his Father.

"I will *watch my ways* so that I do not **SIN WITH MY TONGUE.** I will bridle my mouth while wicked people are in my presence."

Psalm 39:1

Control Your Temper

Anger is an emotion that God allows, but only when it doesn't lead you to sin (see Ephesians 4:26). You can't allow any emotion to lead to sin. That's the key to your emotional life. If your emotions cause you to hurt someone, or if your emotions attempt to control you and convince you to do anything that is sinful, then they have too much power in your life.

Self-control is considered a fruit of the Spirit (see Galatians 5:22–23). That means that it is evidence of your salvation and that it isn't just you alone who makes it happen. You can trust that the Holy Spirit will help you if you are willing to be helped. The bottom line is that you have to keep God in mind whenever your temper starts to flare. A lost temper is a lost opportunity to obey God. When you lose your temper, you lose. If you have trouble with your temper, then try this:

1. **Count to ten before you say a word.** Sometimes just a slight pause in the action allows you to hit the reset button before your CPU overheats. If it doesn't, move on to #2.
2. **Excuse yourself.** Politely tell the other person that you'll get back to them, and get out of the situation. If they press you, say, "I'm really sorry, but I just can't talk about this right now," and walk away.
3. **Do something physical that isn't destructive.** This one works whether you're alone or face-to-face

with your frustration. Run, walk, bike, bowl—just don't punch or slam something. Use the physicality for something constructive and to clear your head.

4. **When all else fails, *pray*.** Yeah, that's sarcasm. This one actually goes hand-in-hand with #1. Pray that God will take your anger and give you perspective. Remind yourself through prayer to love God, your neighbors, and your enemies.

Don't Argue or Fight

The God Guy doesn't argue or fight because he knows that "A servant of the Lord must not quarrel but must be kind to everyone, be able to teach, and be patient with difficult people" (2 Timothy 2:24 NLT). When you fight with someone, you are out of control. Fighting simply means that what others think or do matters so much to you that you have to change them. And the truth is, what others do should never be so important to us that we argue or fight in order to change them. The God Guy knows that he can't change anyone but himself, so fighting is futile. It only makes him look out of control and angry, and it brings no glory to his God.

A SERVANT OF THE QUARREL BUT MUST EVERYONE, BE AND BE PATIENT WITH

106

Don't let disagreement with those you love ever become an excuse to stop loving them. That is to deny God's law and make up your own. The God Guy must love at all times, even when he is hurt, angry, or disagrees with those he loves. It can be really hard to control yourself when you have the urge to fight, but when you do you build your character and you grow in strength. Proverbs 20:3 says, "Avoiding a quarrel is honorable. After all, any stubborn fool can start a fight." Don't be a stubborn fool. Let go and let God deal with the person, and you will show not only your love but your undying trust in the God of the universe.

Control Your Tongue

With our tongues we praise our Lord and Father. Yet, with the same tongues we curse people, who were created in God's likeness. Praise and curses come from the same mouth. My brothers and sisters, this should not happen! Do clean and polluted water flow out of the same spring?

James 3:9–11

LORD MUST NOT BE KIND TO ABLE TO TEACH, DIFFICULT PEOPLE.

The God Guy uses his tongue to praise God, to worship him, to pray to him, and to love him. With it he gives hope to those around him and communicates love to those who will listen. Because of who he is and who he believes in, the God Guy doesn't want his tongue to ever get out of control. When it does, he hurts not only his reputation but the reputation of the God he praises.

You can't be a God Guy and use your tongue for sin. That means you can't use it like a weapon, swinging it all around, knocking people in the head and the heart. You have to use it wisely. Control your urge to let loose on someone who has offended you or hurt you, and instead choose to use your mouth only for good, only for building up. "Don't say anything that would hurt [another person]. Instead, speak only what is good so that you can give help wherever it is needed. That way, what you say will help those who hear you" (Ephesians 4:29).

Your tongue and the words you choose represent the God you serve. So choose them wisely. Here's how:

1. **Don't get revenge.** "Do not say, 'I'll get even with you!' Wait for the LORD, and he will save you." (Proverbs 20:22). When someone hurts you, insults you, or hates you, look to God for your hope. Taking vengeance doesn't get you what you want and only draws you further into pain and darkness. Obedience to God's Word in everything, especially in pain, will give you peace and hope. (See Deuteronomy 11:26–28; Proverbs 28:19.)

2. **Don't brag.** Never use your tongue to brag about yourself (see James 3:14). It sounds awful to those

108

who listen, and you lose any sign of being a Double G.

3. **Don't say anything out of jealousy (James 3:16).** Jealousy is sinful. It doesn't help others, it only accuses God of not loving you enough to give you what He gave them.

You prove your love to God and to the world when you learn to control what you say. The God Guy knows that when he gets to heaven, he's going to have to give an account for every careless word he says (see Matthew 12:36–37). Knowing that gives him the strength to communicate in love. He knows there is more at stake than just being heard. He communicates love and hope, not bitterness and anger. When the God Guy enters a room, people don't run off or avoid him, because he is fun to be around. He uses his thoughts and his words to build up, to honor, and to respect, and in turn he is honored and respected himself.

When you trust God's Word instead of your own abilities to get what you want, and when you believe God hears your every thought and that because of that other people don't have to hear everything you are thinking, you are free. Free to be who you were meant to be. Free from self-obsession and free from having to fight and scrap to get what you want. Learning to communicate in love will set you free to be the best God Guy you can be.

Double G Checklist

Practice sharing your emotions—If you have a hard time talking about how you feel, then it's time to do a little heavy lifting. This week decide who you are going to share with. It doesn't have to be too much or too deep; it just has to be something emotional. It might be that you tell your mom "I love you" as you walk out the door. Or that you tell your pops "Thanks for being there." Find and take advantage of at least three opportunities to consciously share some beneficial emotion with someone in order to make their life better.

Become a giver—One of the best ways to communicate the love of God with the world is by giving to the world where the world has need. So get involved in making the world a better place. Volunteer this month. Look around for a need and get involved. If you can't figure out where to start, get online and google "volunteer opportunities." You'll be able to find all kinds of things you can do in your city. Even if you live in a small town and there is nothing organized to help with, look around your neighborhood and help where you can. Carry groceries for your neighbor lady. Pick up trash at the park. Just don't let another month go by without giving back to the world.

5

A Guy Who Knows Himself

ALL MY LIFE

I wanted to make it in the sports world. That was hard to do in school because my parents enrolled me in school a year early, so I was a year behind all the other guys physically. My freshman year, I was 5' 2" with size 13 feet. I looked like an *L*. I was 5' 5" my sophomore year, 5' 8" my junior year, and 6' 0" my senior year. I'm 6' 2" now. Yeah, late bloomer. So it was pretty awesome my senior year when I started playing volleyball at my high school. I finally had some decent height, and I was pretty good. In fact, even though the university I went to didn't have a varsity program, I played for their men's club team, and we were pretty good. I even got picked up to play for an Athletes in Action U.S. team that played some of the best national teams in South America. I came back from that experience pretty stoked. I had played against some of the best players in the world, alongside guys from Pepperdine, Penn State, and USC. I started to actually entertain thoughts of trying out for the U.S. national team developmental program.

At this same time I started to get involved in my church college group. My college pastor really wanted me to finish my degree, become an intern, and go to seminary to eventually teach and lead other men. He saw more talents in me than just a killer float serve and being a beast on defense.

I was sure my dream of playing volleyball full time was coming true, until one day I shredded my ankle playing Ultimate Frisbee with the college group. Now I was going to miss my tryout window, my girlfriend had broken up with me because her parents didn't think I'd ever be able to provide for her by being a gym rat, and I had to choose between what my mentor saw in me and whatever was left of my dashed dreams. Would I serve God or serve myself and my dream of sports glory and the girl?

I struggled with the throbbing of my shredded ankle in a cast and my shredded dreams in my hands. And unfortunately, I choose option number three. Instead of listening to a trusted mentor or paying attention to my immature ways, I chose to drop out of school and start making cash so I could get the girl. And so I began an almost fifteen-year period of being in the wilderness, running away from who I was to become. Even though in that time I eventually became a head volleyball coach at a large university, it wasn't until I really started to let God teach me about who I am and what I was created for that everything started falling into place.

When I found my "bottom,"

I FINALLY SURRENDERED TO GOD

and said, "Show me who I am and who I am to become," and that was when I began to write. I got a job with the largest Bible software company in the world and started traveling and teaching influential leaders of the faith how to save time and go deeper in their study. Then I met an amazing, godly woman, and we started making bestselling books together. All that came because I wanted to serve God more than I wanted anything else, and I believed him when he said he wanted only the best for me and believed that he would give me the desires of my heart (see Psalm 37:4).

Everyone has dreams, hopes, and fantasies about their life and who they want to be. It's part of growing up and making plans. You have to dream; you have to imagine your life as it could be. There is nothing wrong with that. In fact, it's the job of every God Guy to search himself and his God to know what he was made for and what he will become. I believe who you can become has no limits other than God's limits. And that means that whatever he has planned for you will be amazing and more than you could ever imagine.

The first verse I ever memorized was 2 Corinthians 5:17: "This means that anyone who belongs to Christ has become a new person. The old life is gone; a new life has begun!" (NLT). I've known this verse since I became a Christian, but it's amazing how verses can take on even deeper meaning long after you've first read them. Your new life, no matter what God has planned for you, will blow your socks off if you are willing to be honest with yourself about who he's made you to be. That means that as a God Guy, you have to know yourself: your weaknesses and your strengths, your abilities and your inabilities. You also have to know your danger zones: things you may be chasing after that promise success and hope but are only a cheap imitation of what God really wants for you.

God doesn't leave you

to figure this stuff out on your own. He is right beside you, guiding you and talking to you, if you will only listen. But listening to God isn't always easy when the world is shouting in your ear. When you understand the way God guides you to your purpose, and when you can recognize the sound of his voice, you will more quickly see his plans for you and know where to go next in your journey of life. So let's take a look at some ways that you can get to know yourself better than you do right now.

Know Your Weaknesses

It can be easy to ignore your weaknesses or to say that you don't have any, but you know that is never true. We are all weak in different areas. And those weaknesses should not be feared but recognized (see 2 Corinthians 12:7–10). Being honest about what you can and can't do, where you are weak and where you are strong, is the quickest way to get into line with God's will for your life. Because when you deceive yourself or you let others lie to you, you miss out on the true gifts that are right in front of you.

Weaknesses don't have to be bad things. When you own them and refuse to let them get you down or lie to you anymore, they can be the very thing that gets you to the feet of Jesus. That's because without weakness, you wouldn't need him. So let's take a look at a few signs that point to your weaknesses. See if any of these are showing up in your life. Then thank God for showing them to you.

Guilt

The guilt I'm talking about here is the guilt you feel when you do something wrong. It's a feeling that comes over you when what you do and what you believe don't line up. For a believer, guilt isn't a bad thing; it isn't punishment, for there is no condemnation for those who are in Christ (see Romans 8:1). But it is a sense of knowing, a nudge in your heart that something is wrong, and because of that, feelings of guilt need to be listened to—not fretted over or stewed over but soberly listened to.

When you feel guilty, you have to figure out if it's because of some sin in your life that you haven't given up or confessed. If it is, then you have to stop that sin right away. Sin is weakness; it is the best way to get you away from your purpose. It makes you unsure, unstable, and undirected. In order to know who you truly are, you have to be willing to be honest with yourself about what makes you feel guilty and then have the strength of will to stop the action that leads you there.

Because guilt can be so hard to read—is it real guilt or false guilt?—it's important to find someone who can help you know the difference. Every God Guy should have a mentor or

117

a discipler, someone who knows God's Word and is brave enough to point out your weaknesses and sin yet compassionate enough to help you through the rough parts of life. A great old quote is that a true friend stabs you in the front. That's what a good mentor or discipler will do.

After you identify the sin in your life that is causing all your guilt and you confess it to God with the intention of never doing that thing again, you can be sure that you are no longer guilty (see Psalm 32:5). If you continue to feel guilty after confession and repentance then you are living a lie. The lie is that God isn't big enough to forgive *you*, as if you are some special case. He could forgive murderers, prostitutes and thieves, but not you. See the lie. When you confess and repent you can be sure that you are no longer guilty, and any feeling of guilt you have did not and will never come from God. When you understand God's power to forgive then you have freedom—freedom to be who you were made to be, without all the chains of spiritual confusion and deception. Finding the feelings of guilt in your life instead of ignoring them will help you to better know not only yourself but your God as well. Here's how to start dealing with the guilt in your life:

1. **Listen.** When you read a book like this or hear something someone else says and it makes you feel guilty—listen. The Holy Spirit could be talking to you.

In the vineyard, the vinedresser finds sick vines. Those are the ones that have fallen to the ground and are covered in dirt and mold. These vines can't produce any fruit living down in darkness, so the vinedresser lifts them up and cleans them off. He doesn't chop them off, but he lifts them up so that they can get into the sunlight and start to produce fruit. They are valuable to him and may still be able to be productive when he can get them up off the ground.

FROM A SPIRITUAL PERSPECTIVE, your sin is what makes you sick and dirty and unable to bear fruit. And when that happens, God, the vinedresser, comes along and shakes your world. He scrubs and cleans and moves you to another place.

Do you have some stuff in your past that you have given up—bad stuff, sinful stuff that you have moved past? If you can look back and see a change has come to your life, then you are bearing fruit. The light is coming to you and growth is happening. If you can't look back and see how your life has changed, then maybe it's time to start paying attention to the hand of God in your life. Find out where he's trying to clean you up and lift you up, and stop fighting him.

2. **Investigate the pain.** If something is giving you emotional pain, pay attention to it. Could God be trying to talk to you to get you to see where you are sinning? Not all emotional pain is a sign of guilt, but it's a good place to investigate your holy health. It could be a sign of God's holy discipline (see Proverbs 3:11).

3. **Don't ignore the silence.** You can't find the voice of God if you are ignoring his discipline or his law. Silence in your study time might just mean there is something you need to confess and to get rid of. Take some time to figure out what that could be (Psalm 66:18).

4. **Get over it.** If you have examined your guilt in the light of God's Word and agreed with him by confessing what needs to be confessed and promising not to do it again then the guilt is gone. No more guilt. That means you've got to get over it. Holding onto your guilt is denying the gift of God.

Resentment

In this world people are going to fail, and they are going to fail you. Knowing that, it's up to you to decide how you are going to deal with it when they do. If you hold on to a grudge because of what another person did to you or around you, or if you resent them or their actions, then you've found your weakness.

When a guy has resentment towards someone or even some group, he gives them control of his emotions. And having control of emotions is a powerful position. Resenting someone might feel like strength, like you are taking some kind of a stand, but in fact it is weakness and messes with your life. Resentment can lead to

ANGER, DEPRESSION, stress,
and spiritual stagnation.

If you want to be strong, confident, and going somewhere, then you have to get rid of the resentment that you're holding on to. Whatever someone has done or not done to you should be of no concern. What should be of concern is your relationship with God. You think Christ didn't have something to hold a grudge over? Seriously. You think he shouldn't have been steaming with resentment? But that wasn't his nature at all, was it? And he doesn't want it to be yours. As a Double G, you should stand on what you believe, you should have values and beliefs, but you should never allow other people's values, beliefs, or actions to change who you are or how you act.

When a guy lives with resentment, he thinks things like this: "I'm not good enough," "People are out to get me," "Hard work is a waste of time," "Being 'good' is weakness," "Things will never change," "I will never succeed," "Life isn't fair." Do those sound like thoughts of strength and faith? Of course not. They are the opposite of strength and faith, and they have to go. So if you have resentment in your life, here is what you've got to do:

1. **Get over it.** If someone hurt you but hasn't asked forgiveness, you don't have to forgive them for what they did (see Luke 17:3–4), but you *do* have to get over it. Forgiveness isn't something that God gives to people who don't confess what they've done (see 1 John 1:9), and it isn't something you have to give, but you do have to drop the subject from your heart. You have to decide that you aren't going to keep reliving it or letting it become a part of who you are. Drop the subject in your mind, give it over to God, and promise him that you aren't going to let the other person's mistakes make you bitter or vengeful.

2. **Confess.** Resentment is a sin (see Colossians 3:13). You can't be the judge and jury of the world.

Your job is not to condemn people but to love God and to lead others to him. So it's time to confess your sin and your inability to stop obsessing about someone else's life and start living your own.

3. **Pray.** Prayer will be your way out. You have to pray for the person you resent, and you have to pray for your own humility and strength to get over whatever it was they did.

Repeated Failure

Failure is not a sure sign of weakness. Edison failed almost 10,000 times before inventing the lightbulb. Failure is a necessary part of life, but failure can also be a sign that you are going the wrong direction. If there is something you keep trying but you keep failing at, take a long hard look at yourself. Are you being honest with yourself? Are others saying you should give up what it is you keep failing at? Is God trying to get you to turn around and try another door? Don't let failure get you down, but use it for your good. Either you will

FAILURE IS NOT A SURE SIGN OF WEAKNESS.

grow stronger in the face of it and continue till you succeed, or you will take it as evidence that you don't know yourself well enough and it's time to start looking for more insight from God on where to go next.

Here are some ideas for you when failure is a part of your life:

1. **Get a second opinion.** Failure isn't always bad; sometimes it's good practice for success. But if all you ever do is fail, then maybe it's time to get a second opinion. Ask someone who is smart, wise, and godly if they think you could ever be great at what you are failing at right now. If they say no, then maybe you are seeking something that wasn't meant for you (see Proverbs 12:15).

2. **Get God's help.** If you continue to fail at something, spend some time—not just 15 minutes but hours—talking to God about your strengths and what he wants you to do with your life. Talk out loud, talk in your head, talk by writing it down. However you do it, ask him to open a door for you in this area if it is his will. One door might just be all you need

"If through a broken heart God can bring His purposes to pass in the world, then thank Him for breaking your heart."

Oswald Chambers

to keep going, but if no doors open, then maybe it's time to move on to some other dream.

Procrastination

Do you ever put off doing something that you have to do? Procrastinating is usually the easiest route to take. Procrastination says, "I'm too tired right now," or "That's too hard to do," or "I'll just do it later." It is an attempt to put off responsibility until the last possible moment. You might never have thought of it as a sign of weakness, but when something needs to be done and you deliberately avoid doing it until the last minute, that just shows that you are letting your emotions control your actions. Your emotions say one thing and your body obeys. This is a sign of weakness because it creates a habit in you of doing what is easiest and most comfortable. And ease and comfort are not strong choices; they are not paths to strength of character or of habit.

If you procrastinate, then you need to ask yourself why. Do you procrastinate for any of these reasons?

I am overwhelmed with fear and anxiety.

I'm afraid I will fail.

I'm distracted by other problems.

The task is just boring.

I'm a perfectionist and I won't do it if I won't be the best.

I'm just too busy.

TALK TO GOD

Once you can answer the question "Why do I procrastinate?" you can start to solve the problem. By the way, don't put off asking yourself that question! You have to look at your answer to the question from a spiritual angle. If you are afraid you will fail, then you have to come to terms with the fact that fear should never be what motivates a believer. If you are distracted by other problems, then you might be making those other problems into idols, allowing them to consume you and to control you and your time.

When you've looked into the spiritual cause of your procrastination, talk to God about it and then make a plan for overcoming your weakness. Make a priorities list for yourself. Set goals, and find a way to put things in order so that you can do what needs to be done. If there are distractions in your life, find a way to avoid them or at least to make a space where you can work without distractions. Taking control of your life by refusing to let procrastination control you will give you the spiritual, mental, and emotional strength you are looking for.

All Fun, No Work

All work and no play makes Jack a dull boy, but all fun and no work makes Jack a loser. It's good to have fun, and it's good to get rest from all your hard work and to do things that take your mind off of things, but if fun takes up more than 50 percent of your time (and I'm being generous), then you've found another weakness. I mean, God worked six days and rested on the seventh. So maybe we should say it's a problem if you're playing more than a seventh of your life? Playing is the main occupation of little boys, and work is the main occupation of men. As you move from boyhood to manhood, you make a shift to achieving and providing. If you haven't made or aren't making that shift, then you are still stuck in your boyhood. Don't put off what you could finish today—and I'm not talking about the Nazi Zombie level on Call of Duty 5.

Knowing Yourself, Showing Yourself

Once you know yourself, you have to show yourself. The God Guy is always consistent. He is the same when he's alone as he is with others, and that's why the world sees in him just who he is. He doesn't misrepresent himself or his God. That means that his character, his style, his attitude, his words, and his actions all express his faith. If you are a God Guy, then you will be the same in all these areas.

Character

A man's character is his most valuable asset. Who you are when no one is looking, who you are to people who can't do a thing for you, and the man you will one day become are all based on your character. You can try as hard as you can to hide your true character, but it will always ultimately shine through into the lives of those around you. As a believer your character should never be in conflict with what you believe. If it is, then you have a weakness that needs some attention.

A great and easy to read book on the subject of character and integrity is *Deadly Viper: Character Assassins* written by two guys I know, Mike Foster and Jud Wilhite. I highly encourage you to find a copy or download their audio book. But let me emphasize that character is not a personal thing; it's a community thing. You need guys in your life who you can be totally transparent with and talk about not just your temptations but also when you mess up. Everyone, and I mean *everyone*, has flaws in their character. Having character and integrity doesn't mean that you live a perfect life. Instead it's about creating a lifestyle that protects against your flaws and develops an honest and humble response when you mess up. I could keep going and steal all of Mike and Jud's stuff, but that would show bad character! Go to our social networking site, iFuse.com, and I'll hook you up with all the *Deadly Assassin* protective gear you need.

Attitude

Your attitude is what you think about the things that happen to you and how you show the world the man you are. A bad attitude is like a red flag in the face of the people you are around, and it can knock you down as fast as a right hook. People decide who you are based on your attitude. The way you say what you say and do what you do shows everyone who you really are.

But what if your attitude is bad but your heart is good? Too bad, because no one will know it. All they can judge is what they see. And they can't see your heart. So in order to get the attention of people and help them to know you to be a man they can trust and believe in, you have to show them a good attitude. Being dark, angry, disrespectful, or even shy makes it hard to gain respect, admiration, and the faith of those around you. You might feel all of those things or one of those things in your gut, but you can't let that affect how you act. You have to act based not on your feelings but on your beliefs.

Having a good attitude isn't just a natural result of being a good guy; it can take work. But when you do the work, you get the reward. A good attitude affects the people around you, and it also affects you. We're commanded to think well of others (Philippians 4:8). When you think good thoughts you get good feelings and when you think bad thoughts you just bring all that bad into your life. So change your attitude and you will show yourself to be an authentic Double G.

If you have an attitude problem, here are some ways to fight it:

1. **Start seeing *everyone* as important to God.** As a soldier for Christ, your job isn't to get involved in civilian affairs (see 2 Timothy 2:4) but to carry out your orders. And your orders are to love your neighbor as yourself (see Mark 12:31). So get back on task and stop making your battle plans yourself.

2. **Stop the negativity.** When you complain, even silently, about how stupid something or someone is, it shows in your attitude. So the next time you start to complain to yourself, stop. You can't allow negative thoughts to change who you are, so you have to replace those thoughts with God's Word. Look up at least five verses that make sense to you and say something positive for your mind. Write

them down on something and carry it with you. Look at them every time you start to get negative, and you will change the pattern and overcome your attitude problem.

Style

Your style, as in what you decide to wear today, tells the world what to think about you. People judge other people by how they look, and while you can't change your face, you can change your clothes. As a God Guy it is important that you represent. That means that you don't go around all dirty and messed up. You don't have to be totally stylish or hot, but you should look like you made some effort. You have the power to affect how people look at you and think about you, and because of that you control to some extent how they treat you.

For example, if you are going in for an interview at a business, you aren't going to go in wearing your surf shorts and flip–flops—they'd walk you right out. Clothes are your edge. You have to decide who you want to be and then dress accordingly. In order to get respect where you want and need it, you have to show people who you are on the inside by how you dress on the outside. If you want to start getting more respect, then take a look at your wardrobe and get rid of some things.

131

Stop with the advertising T-shirts that advertise some band or event that you went to. As soon as someone sees you in that, they make a decision about you based not on who you are but on who the advertising is for. This is true for stuff from Abercrombie and other stores as well. If you want to up your odds on impressing people, then make it easier for them by not wearing something they need to read and make a decision about.

ONE OF THE MOST EMBARRASSING BUT helpful **MOMENTS IN MY LIFE** was when I was seventeen and riding my bike everywhere, like a little Greg LeMond (he came before Lance Armstrong). One of my mentors had to write a recommendation for me to work at a youth camp all summer, and under "personal hygiene" he said, "Needs to shower more and use deodorant." Ouch!

Brush your hair. Use pit rub. It sounds simple and even stupid, but if you don't keep the body clean, you aren't going to attract the attention of anyone except the exterminator. A God Guy represents God, and so does his odor.

Getting Physical

A God Guy knows himself, and he knows that looking for loopholes to God's commandments is a slippery slope to destruction. It's easy to look away from truth and to settle somewhere in a gray area where nothing is clear and so everything is okay. But to lie to yourself and to girls about things like how far is too far is to tell the world that God isn't enough for you. It's inconsistent with who you say you are. A God Guy is secure in who he is and knows that God's way is the best way, and because of that he's not willing to compromise and believe that anything short of going "all the way" is okay. When you know yourself as a God Guy, you know that to compromise is to walk away from God.

Getting physical is getting distracted. The more physical you let yourself get, pretending that God doesn't have anything to say about it, the more you are playing with fire. It can be hard to know where God draws the line physically when it comes to girls, but that can't be a reason to do whatever you feel. In order to keep your physical life holy and pure, think about some of these things:

1. **Avoid the guilt.** If what you are doing leaves you feeling guilty, then you are sinning. Stop immediately and confess it to God. "Anything that is not done in faith is sin" (Romans 14:23).

2. **Make a plan.** Decide way before you need to how far is too far. If you have a game plan before things get too hot and heavy, you will be more likely to play it safe.
3. **Get accountable.** Find someone who will ask you the hard questions. When you know you will have to tell someone what you did the night before, you are much less likely to mess up.
4. **Read another book.** One of mine, of course. It's called *Almost Sex: 9 Signs You Are About to Go Too Far (or Already Have)*. It's a good one!

Know Your Strengths

As a God Guy it's important to know yourself well enough to not only know your strengths but also act on them. You are called not to hide your faith but to let it show. Jesus talks about not wasting your gifts and opportunities when he tells the story about the talents (see Matthew 25:14–30).

Your talents might be totally obvious or they might be in hiding, but either way I can tell you

YOUR talents MIGHT BE TOTALLY OBVIOUS

for sure that you have some, no matter how lost you might feel at times. But don't worry; there is hope. When you are searching for yourself, your dreams, and your future, you can do some things that will help you drill down to what's important so that you can take steps in the right direction for you. Most of the time, that's the best part of life—the exploring part. At this time in your life you have more possibilities than you will ever have again. The world is yours to explore.

I remember a time when I was just punching a clock and hating my job. I wanted a change, and I wanted to really enjoy my job and also make a difference in people's lives. So one of the things I did that really helped me to figure out my strengths and my weaknesses was to take some personality tests. There are a ton of them out there, like the Myers-Briggs inventory and others, and you can get a lot of them free online. As you take them you will find out a ton about yourself and hopefully get some info on the way your future will unfold.

If there is something that you really dig, think about finding an internship in that area to see if you really like it once you actually do it. Or try out job shadowing. Do whatever you can to get the information you need to

135

IF THERE IS SOMETHING THAT YOU LOVE AND ARE REALLY GOOD AT, THEN YOU CAN CONSIDER DOING IT AS MINISTRY.

make a good decision about what you want to, or need to, do with your life.

If there is something that you love and are really good at, then you can consider doing it as ministry. Want to be a doc? Then how about going to a country that needs you and serving the poor there? Want to build houses? How about finding a ministry that builds homes for needy people? You can do so many things with your talents, but the one thing you can't do is let them go to waste. You *can* have your work simultaneously be ministry, so do the work it takes to find out where you can invest the gifts God has given you so that your life will be more than you ever thought it could be!

Double G Checklist

Check yourself—Find out if who you think you are is who the world thinks you are. Answer these questions: What are my biggest weaknesses? What are my biggest strengths? Then ask three other people who know you well how they would answer these same questions, and see if there is agreement. If they don't agree with you, take some time to figure out why. Who is right and who is wrong?

Do a self-assessment—Is there anything you've been doing for a long time that leaves you feeling bad, guilty, or stressed? If so, it might be time to call it what it is: a distraction from the main thing, or even a sin. Don't let your busy life crowd out what really counts. So get a piece of paper and write down some things that you think might be things that God wants you to remove from your life. If they are sin or are leading you to sin, cut them out.

Rebuke review—Think about your life over the past five years. Can you remember any rebukes God has sent your way? Any things you were doing that he took away or that you gave up willingly? Think about why and about how much your life has changed since then. Then spend some time thanking God for his love and discipline.

Action inventory—Not sure if your actions are consistent with who you are? Then do an action inventory. Look at the areas of your life below and write down your actions. Need help? Ask your friends how you act in these areas. Then write down how that compares with who you really are. If you find inconsistencies, then it's time to make some changes. Do your research, read books, that help you better understand who God wants you to be, and hopefully you'll get to the bottom of who you want to be and who you were made to be.

Wardrobe—Does your wardrobe reflect your faith?

Friendship—Are there people who hate you, who are afraid of you, or who you hate?

Girls—How do you interact with girls? What kinds of things do you do with them? Check out our books, *B4UD8* and *Almost Sex* for help.

Faith—Do you walk the talk? How does your faith look from the outside? Interview your friends and ask them what they think about your faith.

Talk—How do you talk? Do you cuss? Are you a complainer, sarcastic, or angry? How do your words line up with what you believe?

6

A Guy Who Knows
God

To be a Double G IS PRETTY COOL

because it means that God, the Creator of the universe, the all-powerful, all-knowing King of Kings, has adopted you as his own. He made you his son, his boy, and he is your Father. Think about that for a sec. What a position. It wipes out every other amazing thing in the world with its super-duper amazingness. It's better than Steve Jobs or Bill Gates adopting you!

Don't get me wrong: all in all I had a great dad, but he didn't always get me. He didn't really know all my strengths and certainly didn't know my weaknesses. He didn't know the best way to discipline me or keep me under control. More importantly, my dad didn't know when to just let me go and take a risk. But when I hit rock bottom, feeling sorry for myself because no one really knew the *real* me, I opened my Bible and my heart and realized there was one person who really knew me: Jesus, the Rock, the one who never changes, never leaves, and never stops knowing me and what's best for me. It was like a load was lifted off my back. I wasn't in charge of my destiny. I wasn't lost and alone in darkness. I was connected to him who loves. I was truly *known*, and it was an incredible experience.

He loves you, you know. No matter what you've done. No matter what! Nothing you could have done in the past can keep you from the love of God. Nothing. You are on his mind all the time. Like a proud poppa, he smiles when he sees you, and he waits for your next glance in his direction and for a chance to just hang with you. But he isn't a big teddy bear just waiting passively for your next hug; he is a powerful and perfect God who won't tolerate sin in your life. And that knowledge a lot of the time can become the main thing you think about him. That's why balance is important in the life of the God Guy. You have to be willing to agree with God that sin isn't good for you or for the world, and then you have to accept the love that he freely gives when you turn to him. It's a pretty cool relationship, really. God gives you boundaries that are good for you—boundaries

He loves you, you know. NO MATTER WHAT YOU'VE DONE.

that keep you from falling off the cliff or bumping into the electric fence.

When you reach out and grab God's big old hand and hold on for dear life, things change. Maybe not all at once, but your life gets better. Sure, things are definitely gonna go wrong. People will distract you, toys will entice you, and you will look away from the one who gives you life, but there is always a way back. And even if you don't walk away, I hope you will always want more. More hope, more peace, more love and faith.

The good thing is that God has made a way for you. He has given you what you need to find him and what you need to stay near him. It's just that sometimes you get off track and you need some help getting back to the basics. So how do you come to know him more? How do you keep your focus off of your problems and on your God? Let's have a look.

A God Guy Prays

We are confident that God listens to us if we ask for anything that has his approval. We know that he listens to our requests. So we know that we already have what we ask him for.

1 John 5:14–15

Are you confident that God is listening? Does he pay attention to what you are saying? Is he waiting to give you what you need? How has your prayer life been? Could it be better? Prayer is something that sets the life of the God Guy apart from the rest of the world. He converses with the God of the universe, and God listens. How cool is that? Prayer is your all-access pass to the Father, and because of it your life is stronger and more steady.

WITHOUT PRAYER
you couldn't call yourself a
God Guy.

You can't love a person and refuse to talk to them. Friends talk. It's how you get to know each other. You talk, you listen, and you start to understand each other. Prayer is just you talking with God. And it's what changes your life from ordinary to pretty cool.

But prayer isn't a given. It isn't always natural. Sometimes it can feel like work. Sometimes your mind wanders, your focus draws back to remembering past conversations with people, or planning your day, or worrying about the future. And when that happens, prayer can feel more like an obligation than a reward. But without prayer your life will be bumpy. It will be messy; it will get all wadded up and blurry. It will become out of control and dirty. Prayer draws you back

YEP, PRAYER IS YOUR CONNECTION TO THE CREATOR OF THE WORLD.

to the greater purpose; it reminds you who you are and who he is.

According to God's Word, prayer should be an integral part of your life. In fact, you are supposed to pray continually (see 1 Thessalonians 5:17). Wow, sound impossible? Crazy even? Well, it's actually not. Think it about it like this: prayer is your mind being hooked up to God's. It's always remembering he is closer to you than your own skin and never forgetting how much he cares and how much he can do in the life of a guy who will let him. God promises to listen to the ones who love him. "He listens to people who are devout and who do what he wants" (John 9:31). And you can also be sure that if you live in him and what he says lives in you, then you can ask for anything you want, and it will be yours (see John 15:7).

Yep, prayer is your connection to the Creator of the world. But sometimes that very fact can make it seem impossible. What do you say? How do you talk? Does he listen? The cool thing is *yes, he does*. He listens to his people. And if you're a God Guy, that's you. But prayer requires a few things of you. So check it out.

Prayer Requires Faith

You can't pray to a God you don't believe in. That would be insanity. So you have to believe he is who he says he is. If you don't, then you can be sure he isn't listening. "No one can please God without faith. Whoever goes to God must believe that God exists and that he rewards those who seek him" (Hebrews 11:6).

Prayer Requires Godly Motives

God knows all your thoughts. He knows your motives—why you ask for what you ask for—so there's no pulling the wool over his eyes. When it comes to asking God for things, your heart has to be set on godliness, not your own wants. Prayers can go unanswered for all kinds of reasons, but one of them could be that what you are asking for isn't something that you want in order to know God more or to draw closer to him but is something you want to get or do to make yourself feel good. Think about some of the things you ask for. Are you asking for them so they can make you happy or complete? Isn't that God's job? Consider why you ask for things, and then focus on the things that please God—the things that make your relationship with him better rather than your life more fun. "When you pray for things, you don't get them because you want them for the wrong reason—for your own pleasure" (James 4:3).

"*Praise* the word of God.
I *trust* God.
I am **NOT AFRAID**.

What can mere
flesh [and blood]
do to me?"

Psalm 56:4

Prayer Requires Patience

King David knew prayer. He was always praying, always calling out to God to help him and protect him, so you could say that he was experienced in the stuff of prayer. He knew that prayers weren't always answered on his timeline, so he got good at waiting. "I waited patiently for the LORD. He turned to me and heard my cry for help" (Psalm 40:1). That patience came out of an understanding that God would get to it when it was best gotten to.

For years and years I wanted God to answer my prayer for the perfect woman. I wanted to find the woman who would laugh at my jokes but better yet, let me be myself. And I couldn't understand why God didn't seem to be listening. It wasn't until years later that I fully understood that I wasn't ready for love and neither were most of the women I chose. Time had to do its work, but I didn't let it. I rushed God and took charge of things for myself, and I got married and divorced all in my early twenties. More than hating that I "married the wrong girl" or that I "didn't wait for the one," I hate that I wasn't man enough to say, "I got into this and now I'm going to see it through." I'm telling you this so you can learn this lesson much sooner than I did. I was never good at patience when I was living for myself. And prayer requires patience, and patience comes from a belief that God has everything under control—even your dreams and your hopes.

147

Prayer Requires Trust

Sometimes God answers your prayers with a big no. But no isn't a bad thing when it comes from God. Nothing bad comes from God. So you can be sure that when you pray and God doesn't answer the way you want, something better is coming.

"GLORY BELONGS TO GOD, WHOSE POWER IS AT WORK IN US. BY THIS POWER HE CAN DO INFINITELY MORE THAN WE CAN ASK OR IMAGINE" (Ephesians 3:20).

As a God Guy you can know beyond a shadow of a doubt that God has only the best planned for you. A great verse is Jeremiah 29:11: "I know the plans that I have for you, declares the LORD. They are plans for peace and not disaster, plans to give you a future filled with hope." If you can trust God's words, then you can trust him with your prayers, no matter what the answer.

Prayer Requires Confession

A guy first comes to know God through an awareness that he isn't perfect, that he's messed up and needs God to pull him up off of the ground. At that moment the clouds open up and things start to become clearer. Confession—agreeing with God that he is right and

"**God** is faithful and reliable. If we confess our sins, he forgives them and cleanses us from everything we've done wrong."

1 JOHN 1:9

your sin is wrong—brings a sigh of relief. It can be embarrassing and hard to get to the point of confessing your messed-up life, but once you can get it out and get through it, you find such relief.

When you confess and turn away from that sin, the worry and stress are all lifted. Confession cleans you. It is simply saying that you are bad and that you can't do this life thing on your own. Confessing that you were wrong and God was right and that you want to make him the Lord of your life is what first brings you to salvation. Without confession you wouldn't be a God Guy.

The daily practice of confession will keep you on track. When every morning you wake up and get real with God, when you don't hide anything, when you agree that you've done this and this and this wrong, you get stronger and stronger. Sin doesn't like to hang around when it knows that it's going to get ratted on. As a God Guy, you should make confession part of your daily routine so you're regularly getting everything out and agreeing with God that it was wrong. Confession is the beginning of prayer; it is a cleaning of the slate. So find time each day to be honest with God and with yourself. This is the start of knowing God and yourself and drawing your heart into a more holy life.

2 THINGS
GOD WON'T DO
WHEN YOU SIN:

- discipline you just to be mean or spiteful or because life has been going too good for you and now it's time for some discipline
- hurt someone else to teach you a lesson—ever!

3 Things
GOD WILL DO
WHEN YOU SIN:

- discipline you when you do something wrong
- do what he can to show you your mistakes in order to get you out of the darkness
- accept your apology every time, anytime, forever

Prayer Requires Adoration

My prayer life was getting boring. I was doing the same thing every morning: going down my list of people and things to pray for and about. I was talking to God about me, and it was flat. Then I tried something I remembered from back in college, and it worked. And when I say it worked, I mean it changed my life. Not only did my prayers get better but my life got better. I got happier. And all because I start out every morning in adoration.

I focus all my mind on adoring God. I look out at every situation he's delivered me from and everything he's worked together for good, and I tell him he rocks. I thank him for his consistency, his power, his grace. I just tell him everything that I love about him. And sometimes I can't stop talking about how incredible he is. You know how it feels when someone goes on and on about how amazing you are? I hope you've experienced that. It's so good. And I want the God of the universe to know that I notice, so I go on and on about how great he is. I try to never be at a loss. And as I verbally confirm what my heart has always known, I release everything awful and ugly from my life. I refocus on what is true and good, and I am drawn

"Every good present and every perfect gift comes from above, from the Father who made the sun, moon, and stars. The Father doesn't change like the shifting shadows produced by the sun and the moon."

James 1:17

into his majesty. I become a part of his whole. And I finally feel peace sitting with the one true God.

Adoration will pour rocket fuel on your prayer life and even on your walking around life. I know from experience that when I skip adoration, my day will be unhappy. My focus will be off, and I won't find my groove. But when I start every day with adoration, I get pumped for what the day is going to bring. It fills my veins like adrenaline, and I am stoked. Life is good when you remember and say out loud that God is good too.

Prayer Requires Worship

HOLY, HOLY, HOLY IS THE LORD OF ARMIES! THE WHOLE EARTH IS FILLED WITH HIS GLORY.

Isaiah 6:3

When you worship God, you get outside of yourself. Your problems and your worries all become miniscule compared to the amazing power and love of God.

grace: the dimension of divine activity that enables God to confront human indifference and rebellion with an inexhaustible capacity to forgive and to bless. God is gracious in action.

Tyndale Bible Dictionary

Worship gives God what he deserves: your undying attention and adoration.

Worship doesn't have to be about music, but most of the time that's what people think of. With music that expresses the goodness and power of God, you draw into worship and come closer to God than to any human on earth. The God Guy is different from the rest of the world because of who he worships. Your salvation, your eternity rests on the fact that you worship God and his Son Jesus Christ.

My prayer life is enhanced when I wake up and put on my favorite worship songs. As I sing or hum along with the words that express his greatness, I am lifted out of the everyday life and raised up to a higher view of things. And it is in that worship that I can truly express to God how important he is to me.

But worship doesn't require music. You can worship God by just doing what he asks you to do. Obedience is worship. You can worship him by serving others, by refusing to break and give in to the world. Worship is more than just tunes; it's your lifestyle, what you do each day with the fact that Jesus died on the cross for you.

Prayer Requires Thanksgiving

Another way to get your prayer and your life back on track with God is to get thankful. It's impossible to be thankful and depressed at the same time. Thankfulness

"The initiative of the saint is not towards self-realization, but towards knowing Jesus Christ. The spiritual saint ever believes circumstances to be haphazard, or thinks of his life as secular and sacred; he sees everything he is dumped down in as the means of securing the knowledge of Jesus Christ. There is a reckless abandonment about him."

Oswald Chambers

is freedom. Complaining is bondage. It ties you down to the cares of this world and distracts you from true beauty. Make it a regular part of your day to give God thanks for all the good things in your life. Nothing is too mundane or silly. Everything you have that is good is from him, so thank him for it.

Prayer is an amazing thing. It gives life to your soul and freedom to your mind. Accept prayer as your daily devotion to God, your proof that he is yours and you are his, the branch of his vine, and you will be a true Double G. Prayer isn't something that you perfect in one day, however; it takes a lifetime to learn its power and its ways. So take slow, deliberate steps and keep your eye on him, and you'll soon be rockin'. But if you do stumble in your prayer life, don't freak. Just get back up again and back into conversation with the one true God.

A God Guy Is Saved by Grace

I can remember how when my dad was on his death-bed, I looked at all the sin in my life and felt ashamed. I was bothered by all my missteps and bad choices. I actually confided this to my dad as he was lying there, days away from death. I said, "I'm sorry most of my life I was a lazy screwup." He said, "Forget that. I'm proud of you. That's in the past." And to this day it still gets me. It was an amazing gift he gave to me. And it's even more astounding to think about, but all your sin is forgivable. It is all covered under the grace of God. And because of that, you can be a confident God Guy who fearlessly walks into your Father's presence, talks with him, shares your heart and mind, and listens to everything the Father has to say.

Consider these words written to you:

BUT BECAUSE OF HIS GREAT LOVE FOR US (you), GOD, WHO IS RICH IN MERCY, MADE US (you) ALIVE WITH CHRIST EVEN WHEN WE (you) WERE DEAD IN TRANSGRESSIONS—IT IS BY GRACE YOU HAVE BEEN SAVED.

Ephesians 2:4–6 NIV

Grace reaches down and says, "I don't care how ugly, mean, or sinful you are or how bad you've been—I love you, and if you will confess your mess-ups and then accept my forgiveness, it will be yours." Grace removes the stains from your life and makes you pure again.

Dude, God loved you before you were lovable, and he loved you enough to do the unthinkable. "He who did not spare his own Son, but gave him up for us all—how will he not also, along with him, graciously give us all things?" (Romans 8:32 NIV). You can expect nothing but the best from God. When times look dark and prayers seem unanswered, you have to hold on tight to the fact that God has it covered. He won't let anyone pull you from his hands, and he knows you can handle everything he allows to happen to you. By trusting in that fact and refusing to doubt it, you will be able to overcome even the most heinous of circumstances. God's grace is enough.

A God Guy Studies

The God Guy is the luckiest guy in the world, because he doesn't have a hidden God or a dead God but has a living God who is willing and eager to communicate with his creation. Through prayer and the acceptance of his grace and forgiveness, the God Guy can get closer to him, but one thing gets him even closer: studying his Word, the Bible. When you open up your Bible and start to read the words in it, they come to life. You can read it over and over again, and each reading gives you just what you need to improve your spirit and your mind.

Reading the Bible used to be a chore for me, until I learned it was like if my earthly father wrote everything he knew about life and me and how I can make it through to the finish line and put it into a book. Not only that, but the book told me all about his character before I even knew him. Once I had that picture in my mind, I knew that if I really wanted to know God and why he created me, I had to read his book. I mean, you've got to—your mind won't let you rest till you do. You crave the answers, the truth about life, and so you study. But studying can get tough after a time. You've read it all before, and now you don't know what to do next, or you can't decide where to start. Studying doesn't always come naturally to all of us, and although you really want to know more about God, you might not know how to go about it. So let me help you out with some ways I've succeeded in discovering the truth in God's Word on a daily basis.

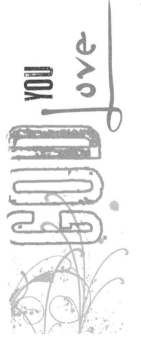

The goal—The goal for your study time should be to find out more about the God that you love. Find out what he likes and dislikes and how he acts, sounds, or interacts. When all you want to know is who he is and what he wants, your study time becomes a lot more directed and manageable.

Research—For me, the best time in study is the time when I am researching a book or a talk I'm going to give to other men. I have a topic all picked out, like risk or fear or sex. Whatever the topic is, I start to research all that

God has to say about it. I open up a concordance or I look up the topic online or in my Bible software, and I start to climb. I move from one verse to the next, and then that takes me to another idea that is connected to my main topic. And as I work I write down what I am learning. I write small paragraphs on each topic and fill them out with a bunch of verses that support the idea. I work to make a case for whatever it is I am researching. As I do, the Bible starts to come to life, and so does my study time. It's as if the Bible is a bottomless cave of priceless gems and experiences. I can never draw all there is to draw out of it. If you want your study to come to life, consider drilling into a topic as I do when I write a book. It will help you to learn more than you ever knew and to stay focused on the job at hand.

The Tools—In order to really dive into Bible study, you have to have the tools needed. First is a good translation. Consider one that you can understand easily, something readable like the GOD'S WORD translation or the New Living Translation. Something that makes sense to you. If words don't scare you and you want a translation that's more majestic and tries to translate word-for-word instead of thought-for-thought, give the English Standard Version a look. Then find some reference works like a Bible handbook or a concordance. If you don't have them at home, you can always look online for Bible tools like an online concordance or a searchable Bible. Places like BibleGateway.com, Bible.Logos.com, and Crosswalk.com have a number of helpful online tools. You can also just type the topic you are studying into a search engine and see what you can find. But bring it all back to your Bible. Don't take other people's word for it. Find out how what they are saying lines up with Scripture. And if you still aren't sure, keep researching. Here are some sample sources (some free, some not) for your studying tools:

Strong's Concordance
Bible Knowledge Commentary
Believers Bible Commentary
New American Commentary
New Topical Textbook
Where to Find It in the Bible
Illustrated Manners and Customs
Any good Bible dictionary

You can also go to your pastor and find out what commentaries and reference works he uses.

When you want more of God—more of his grace, his peace, and his hope—you have to be willing to do some heavy lifting. You can't just wait for it to come to you through osmosis by sleeping with the Bible under your pillow. You have to be willing to do the work. Read the words, find out what you need to know, and don't rely on others. Sure, others can help guide you and get you started, but ultimately you are responsible for knowing why you believe what you believe. You are old enough and smart enough to do this. You can dive into God's Word like anyone else. You can find out what God wants of you and what would make him happy. You can feel closer to him and less stressed out by life if you will only open up his Word each day and do a little work. Read a little, search a little, learn your way around your faith, and your life will continue to improve.

THE GOD GUY IS A STUDENT OF HIS GOD.

He takes nothing for granted but does all he can to find out who God is and how he loves. The God Guy stays connected to God through prayer and study. He worships him freely, adores him, and agrees with him when he messes up. The God Guy knows himself because he knows the God who created and purposed him for good works. He communicates in love and knows the secret to true happiness is found in loving him. And he finds love all over the place because he sees the world through God's eyes. He gives love—not to get it back but to share that which his God has given him. The Double G is a breath of fresh air to a perishing world. He rises above circumstance and finds peace in the turmoil because he trusts. His life may be in chaos, but his heart is calm and strong because of where he has his focus.

The God Guy is the best guy you can be. He is you when you accept Christ and yourself and when you want to be better but for now are happy with who you are. He is who you were meant to be, a child of God, deeply loved by God, who calls you his son. The God Guy is the meat of your soul. Take heart in your position and find hope in his love. You are a God Guy and you are God's.

Double G Checklist

Pray about it—This week pray the same thing every day: "God, show me the sin in my life. And if the hard times I'm experiencing aren't because of sin, then show me that you are just pruning away the good to get to the best." Then listen. Listen each day. Study his Word and see what comes to you so that you can determine what needs to be cut out of your life and why.

Concentration cards—Don't let your prayers get distracted. Practice concentration. That means constantly putting your thoughts back onto God, even though they wander. Don't get upset; just put them back on him when you feel a drift. To help with this, make concentration cards. Get some 3-by-5 cards or Post-it notes and write out the things you want to pray about or concentrate on in your prayer time. Then keep them in front of you as you start to pray. Look at them often so you don't get off track and drift into thinking about the last fight you had with your friend or what you are going to do Friday night. Make a list like this: confess, adore, thank him, pray for Mom/Dad/job, etc. The concentration cards will keep you more focused than just letting your prayer wander.

Thank-you list—Wanna really thank God for everything? Then sit down and write a thank-you list. Think of everything, and I mean everything, that you are thankful for. Your car, TV, a roof over your head, your parents, your dog, Jesus, your church, the Bible, forgiveness, everything. Not just super spiritual stuff but everything good. It all comes from him.

HAVE YOU THANKED HIM LATELY FOR IT?

Create a verse list—A verse list is just a list of verses on a particular subject, kind of like a concordance. Have you ever said, "Man, I wish I could remember that verse that was so good"? Well, this verse list will help you to keep those kinds of things close to your eyes and your heart. So here's how you make one: make a list of all the things you want to know about God and your life. Things like salvation, leadership, love, sex, fighting, and so on. Then look up every verse you can find on it that connects with you. Write the verses down or type them up next to each topic. Then when you are looking for the verse you need, you'll be able to find it quickly. You'll also be able to use your list for a devotional. Need help on worry today? Go to your list of verses on worry and read them all. A verse list is a great way to learn God's Word and find your way into it quickly.

A Final Word to the
God Guy

BEING A GOD GUY
is the most *heroic*
and **POWERFUL** thing
you will ever be.

When you decide that God's Word alone defines who you are and what you do, you find everything you need for life, hope and for peace. God defines the God Guy because he is his. God first, guy second. He belongs to him, serves him and loves him. To those who don't get it, you might seem out of touch with the world, but take heart, you aren't out of touch, you are just out of agreement. The world doesn't define the God Guy (that would be a "World Guy"). He doesn't take its ideas of good and bad and make them his own, but he examines everything he reads, hears and sees through the light of God and his Word.

Being a God Guy will change you, every day. In everything you do, you will find more happiness and direction because your will will be in line with his. Pastor James MacDonald puts it this way, "if your faith isn't changing you, it hasn't saved you." To a lot of people that sounds like bad news or heavy lifting. But to the God Guy that sounds like confirmation that his life is on the right track. When you are constantly improving, constantly agreeing with God that your way of thinking or acting is wrong and making the proper adjustments you will see amazing changes in your life, your confidence, your peace and your hope.

It is my prayer that none of this should overwhelm you but instead give you a sense of excitement and adventure. Even if you look at your life in disgust you should be encouraged, because those who are really the worst off are those who see nothing wrong with the sin in their lives. There is great strength to be found in calling sin, sin, and that strength is in the knowledge that all sin can be rejected not only by you but by the God who you have invited into your life. With help like that how can you lose? The presence of sin in your life just proves how much you need the God who saves. Be encouraged my brother, and find the strength and hope to change not only your life with this information, but the lives of those around you as well.

Log on to www.ifuse.com to talk to more Double Gs like yourself and to ask me questions. I look forward to seeing you there.

Michael

Michael DiMarco is the CEO of Hungry Planet, a company that creates cutting-edge books to connect with the multitasking mind-set. He has also held positions as Chief Marketing & Creative Strategist for Teen Mania, university volleyball coach, morning show DJ, and host of a humor and advice radio program called "Babble of the Sexes." Michael has written or co-written a number of books on relationships, including *Almost Sex, Marriable, The Art of Rejection, The Art of the First Date*, and *B4UD8*.

Continue your *God Guy* journey
with this year-long daily devotional

Available wherever books and ebooks are sold.